THE SUBURBANIZATION OF NEW YORK

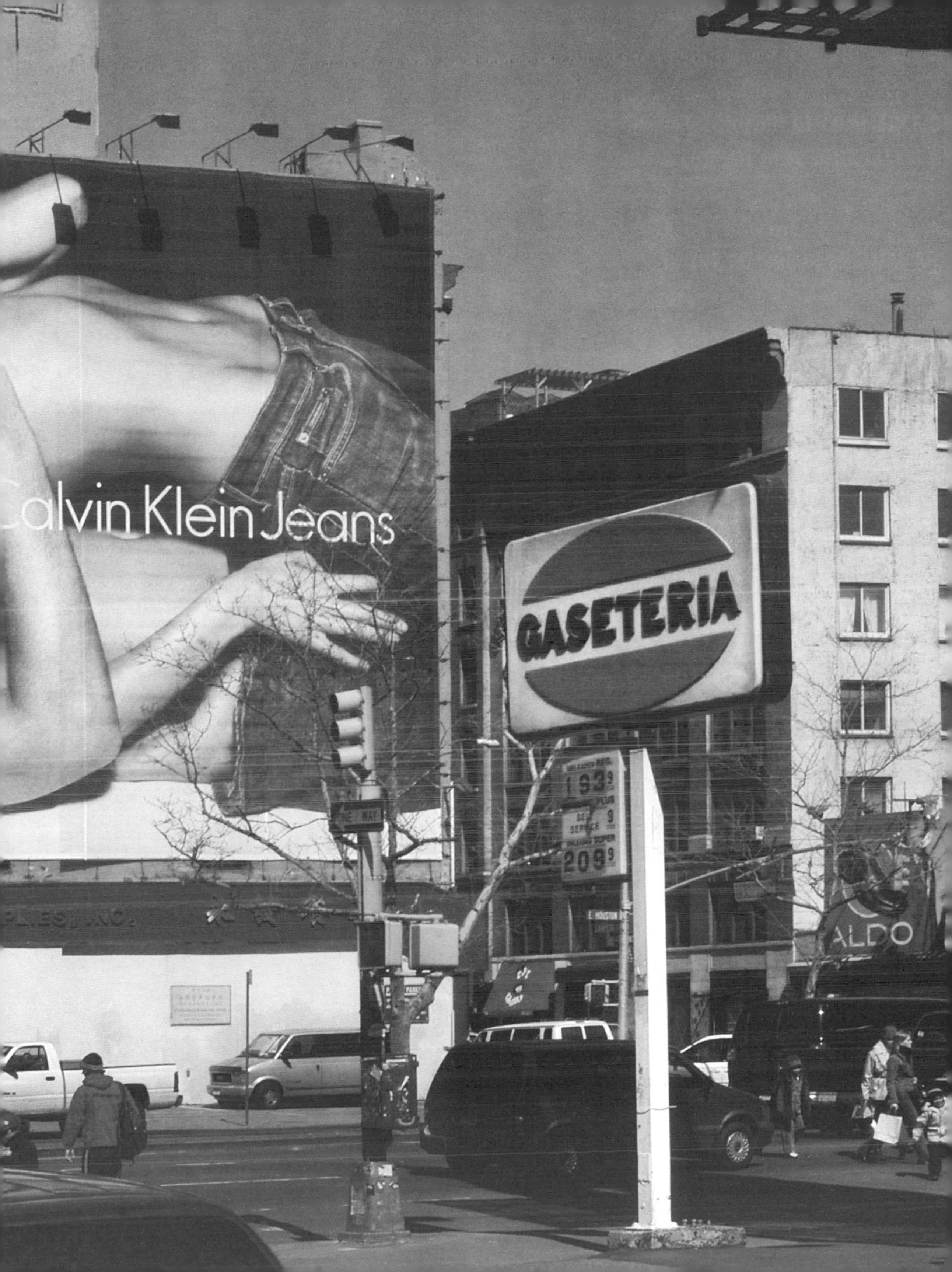

Calvin Klein Jeans
GASETERIA
193 9
209 9
ALDO

THE SUBURBANIZATION OF NEW YORK

Is the World's Greatest City Becoming Just Another Town?

Jerilou Hammett and Kingsley Hammett, editors

Photographs by Martha Cooper

Princeton Architectural Press, New York

Published by
Princeton Architectural Press
37 East Seventh Street
New York, New York 10003

For a free catalog of books, call 1.800.722.6657.
Visit our Web site at www.papress.com.

The Suburbanization of New York: Is the World's Greatest City Becoming Just Another Town? was made possible through the support of the Graham Foundation for Advanced Studies in the Fine Arts and a Furthermore Grant in Publishing from the J. M. Kaplan Fund.

Project Editor and Proofreader: Linda Lee
Acquisitions Editor: Clare Jacobson
Designer: Jan Haux

Special thanks to: Nettie Aljian, Sara Bader, Dorothy Ball, Nicola Bednarek, Janet Behning, Becca Casbon, Penny (Yuen Pik) Chu, Russell Fernandez, Pete Fitzpatrick, Wendy Fuller, Sara Hart, Clare Jacobson, John King, Mark Lamster, Nancy Eklund Later, Katharine Myers, Lauren Nelson, Scott Tennent, Jennifer Thompson, Paul Wagner, Joseph Weston, and Deb Wood of Princeton Architectural Press —Kevin C. Lippert, publisher

Library of Congress Cataloging-in-Publication Data
The suburbanization of New York : is the world's greatest city becoming just another town? / Jerilou Hammett and Kingsley Hammett, editors ; photographs by Martha Cooper.
     p. cm.
 ISBN-13: 978-1-56898-678-4 (pbk. : alk. paper)
 ISBN-10: 1-56898-678-5 (pbk. : alk. paper)
 1. New York (N.Y.)—Social conditions. 2. Gentrification—New York (State)—New York 3. Neighborhood—New York (State)—New York. I. Hammett, Jerilou. II. Hammett, Kingsley H. III. Cooper, Martha.
 HN80.N5S83 2007
 307.3′416097471—dc22

                                                                          2006019851

This book is dedicated to New York, the greatest city in the world.

Contents

What's next for New York? Is it cooking or cooling? Brimming with vitality or sinking into somnolence? Will it retain its edgy preeminence as global crucible, the place par excellence where the world's peoples come to clash and fuse and create the future? Will the forces of suburbanization—now sprawling and malling their way into town—tame the raucous metropolis, subdue its contrarian politics, make of it just another outlet for Disneyfied culture, big-box commerce, and franchise food? Or is something altogether new busy being born at the contested urban-suburban frontier? Only two things are sure: New York is in rapid motion, and this book is a great guide to where it might be headed. Its diverse array of observations—written by some of the country's smartest (and wittiest) analysts and activists—are incisive and accessible, provocative and entertaining, perfect for an urban studies course and for anyone interested in pondering the past and future of cities.

—*Mike Wallace*
Pulitzer Prize-winning co-author of
Gotham: A History of New York City to 1898

Preface

In the eyes of the world, New York has always been the quintessential city: culturally, ethnically, and economically mixed, exciting and chaotic, elusive and spontaneous, sophisticated and endlessly creative. The essential New York had an indefinable complexity; it produced a physical environment that supported a variety of scales and densities and a fine-grained mix of land uses. Creative window displays, exciting colors, and inventive signage made for endless individual expression, and streets pulsated with pedestrian activity around the clock.

For some time now, things have been moving in another direction, as New York, like other cities across the country, has become more suburbanized. It has been more than twenty years since Mayor Koch declared, "We're not catering to the poor anymore...there are four other boroughs they can live in. They don't have to live in Manhattan." With that attitude, a new image began to take hold in New York City as it tried to shed its gritty past and sought to lure back the middle- and upper-class suburbanites who had fled the unruly metropolis. At the same time, larger economic forces such as globalization, the proliferation of franchises, the dominance of national chains, and the omnipresence of corporate branding have challenged the uniqueness and scale of the city's richly woven fabric.

Nowhere is this transformation more dramatically visible than in Times Square. This once varied and raucous theater district has become a giant corporate theme park. Whole buildings act as seven-story electronic billboards, blocking whatever structures stand behind. Megastores have moved beyond emporiums to become entertainment destinations in and of themselves. The overpowering enormity of it all has reduced the pedestrian to a mere supporting role.

The historic South Street Seaport area once attested to the city's role as a major player in world maritime commerce. Today it has become a "festival marketplace" tied to a new brick multilevel indoor mall filled with branches of expensive national tog shops and franchise restaurants.

The forces of gentrification are turning Harlem's 125th Street, for nearly a century the heart of black America, into an outpost of corporate America with gleaming office towers and big-box stores. And a stretch of abandoned Hudson River docks that once served the luxury steamers of the Cunard and White Star lines has been converted into the huge Chelsea Piers recreational complex, what architecture critic Paul Goldberger has called "the mother church of suburbanization." Built to enormous horizontal scale with blank facades fronting the public domain, it symbolizes a new use of suburban forms in the urban landscape. Sheltered within are two ice-skating rinks, a large rock-climbing wall, basketball courts, a gymnastics center, a bowling alley, a roller rink, a driving range, and numerous gyms, including one with a sand-pit floor to accommodate beach volleyball, all served by a 400-car parking lot right off the West Side Highway.

The move from smaller, diverse, neighborhood-scale stores to the tedious ubiquity of predictable and bland national chains is altering the physical environment of New York. The quirky, odd shops, richly textured buildings, and unusual characters that gave the city its distinctive urban glow are disappearing. Giant corporate retailers have consolidated whole market segments—from books to office supplies to pharmaceuticals to hardware—forcing countless independently owned stores to close.

Following the deindustrialization of the city, manufacturing spaces evolved into expensive art galleries, chic restaurants, and trendy boutiques as well as enormously expensive loft apartments. Anxious to attract wealthy tourists and new residents, the city had to offer them what was safe, easy, and familiar. That called for the sanitization of public spaces, the creation of new upscale residential enclaves, the formation of private improvement districts to cleanse areas of unpleasant and undesirable features, and the gentrification of even the most marginal neighborhoods.

Today New York is on its way to becoming a "theme-park city," where people can get the illusion of the urban experience without the diversity, spontaneity, and unpredictability that have always been its hallmarks. Like the suburbs New Yorkers so long snubbed, the city is becoming more private, more predictable, and more homogenized.

What does the future hold for the legendary metropolis, a gateway for immigrants and strivers, a magnet for builders and dealers, and a muse for artists and dreamers? What will happen to once-unique streets that are awash in generic stores, apartment boxes, and garish signs and billboards? Or to the legendary neighborhoods—Little Italy, Hell's Kitchen, Harlem, the Lower East Side—that are now simply real estate markets smoothed over with cute monikers, all equally safe for investment? The essays and photographs in this book explore the rapid changes and mounting challenges facing the city with insight, wit, passion, and a historic perspective that will contribute to an ongoing debate about the present and future of New York.

LOVE AND LOSS IN NEW YORK CITY

Maggie Wrigley

I came to New York in 1984. I landed on the isle of Manhattan new, naïve, and instantly besotted with the gorgeous mayhem of this crazy metropolis. It was dirty and dangerous but full of life, language, color, and action.

The confusion of the subway—that wonderful mess of black, white, and brown, rich and poor, and itinerant musicians—immediately separated me from my only friend ("Is this the stop? yes? no?") as the train doors closed and drove her to parts unknown. Bar a mugging, it was the ultimate welcome to New York.

We were both pleased, though—she, a Jamaican dressmaker, landed in the discount fabric district, which was Broadway below Houston; I, a little rocker, had gotten off at Astor Place, the gateway to St. Mark's Place that ran from punk fashion mecca Trash and Vaudeville down to the gathering yard of Tompkins Square Park, land of the punk poets.

The city was a thrill of neighborhoods, with appropriately thrilling names—Hell's Kitchen, Lower East Side (Loisaida), Alphabet City (the avenues christened, only half jokingly, Adventurous, Brave, Courageous, and Death. After seventeen years I still live between Courageous and Death, though the names have lost their sting).

Every foray brought new sights within the city: The cast iron warehouses and art galleries of SoHo. Little Italy with wise guys outside social clubs, grandmothers and grandbabies sitting on beach chairs by the bakeries, butcher shops, and red sauce restaurants. You could see the bullet holes of a mob rubout in the kitchen door of the old Umberto's Clam House. The stink and stagger of the Bowery, its missions and flophouse hotels marking salvation alley (or end of the line) for the bums and winos, lost souls of drugs and alcohol. The crowded streets and dark alleys of Chinatown, teeming with restaurants with indecipherable menus, and misty sunrise parks full of old and young moving silently in tai chi.

The deafening barrage of firecrackers that had the streets shrouded in smoke and ankle-deep in red paper for the Chinese New Year. The skyscraper caverns of Wall Street and the impossibly high gleaming Twin Towers. To walk this city was to constantly turn corners into new worlds.

The jewelry district around Forty-eighth Street, full of Hasids with locks, hats, and robes and diamonds in their pockets, working in cluttered cubicles glittering with fortunes in jewels. The fashion blocks in Midtown, swirling with racks of clothing pushed through the streets at a furious pace. The garden district in the twenties, the sidewalks sweet-smelling jungles of palm and ficus, palettes of pansies, and stacks of turf. Headstone carvers around Houston Street. Flea markets spread across the city from parking lots on Canal Street to the twenties, Upper West Side, and Harlem. The thieves' markets that sprung up every night around Astor Place and Second Avenue by St. Marks Place—where my friend bought back his leather jacket stolen earlier that night from CBGBs. The densely packed Indian restaurants and spice stores on and around Sixth Street. The swish and shriek of drag queens and leather boys through Christopher Street and the fiercely gay West Village.

The slimy sidewalks of the Meatpacking District and the Fulton Fish Market—west side avenues full of bloody-aproned workers and meat carcasses swinging on hooks from the awnings; on the east side the furious predawn activity of fishmongers tossing tuna and carp, octopus and cod among the early-shopping chefs of the highest and the humblest city restaurants.

The East Village was heavily Eastern European—storefronts housing Jewish hat makers and tailors, butchers and bakers. Ukrainian bars with ancient barmaids, Polish diners fragrant with borscht and stuffed cabbage and open all night, bakeries selling poppy-seed babka and sweet braided challah bread.

The Lower East Side with its grand decaying synagogues, storefront temples now Spanish churches with a different congregation each day of the week. The Jewish merchants with pickle shops or bialys and bagels baked to sell across the city. Orchard Street with fabric stores and hat shops, selling wigs, leather coats, and demure underthings.

The thrill of seeing a freshly graffitied train roll into dirty, dark Times Square as, Claes Oldenburg said, "brightens the place like a big bouquet from Latin America."

Forty-second Street seemed to exist only at night, sodden with sex shops, pinball arcades, and triple-feature all-night theaters; hookers young and old, male and female, and all in between; drug hustlers and the kung fu movie house—cut through by the well-dressed theater patrons headed for the nearby Broadway musicals. Buy a bag of weed and you would have to go back to replace the switched bag of shake and stems. There were three-card-monte street scams, evangelists and fake nuns, "blind" pickpockets.

Uptown to 125th Street—so poor and blighted by drugs, but the city's heart of black history. The smell of soul food and frying fish. Church ladies in gorgeous hats. Crackheads and young toughs. Vendors selling mud cloth hats and kente scarves, incense and shea butter, Masai bracelets and mix tapes, Ivory Coast brass figurines and Ethiopian silver. Mr. Ralston grew tomatoes in his garden dubbed "Black Thumb." I saw James Baldwin one morning on East 131st Street, where he had once lived. Harlem rocked to the hip-hop beat, carried on b-boy shoulders through giant boom boxes downtown on the subways to Washington Square Park and the clubs. Break dancers spun through the city, styling in track suits and Adidas, Kangol hats and gold chains. The girls wore gold earrings big as bricks.

The clubs! Downtown was home to the Mudd Club, Danceteria, the Ritz, Reggae Lounge, CBGBs, Tramps, the Pyramid, A7, Paradise Garage. There were amazing numbers of storefront and basement after-hours clubs, the music and the people running the gamut of our Alphabet City scene. The most famous and long-lived was Save the Robots, subterranean dance hall, gathering house for every stripe of partygoer—black and white; gay and straight; punks, rastas, rockers, club kids, and drag queens; Hells Angels and hustlers. Dancing until noon unless a police raid forced them all out stumbling and blinking into the morning sunlight. Scorpio was a dark cavern. Torys an Italian chrome palace. Del Montes had live bands, go-go dancers on the bar, and ever-changing decor courtesy of local artists. Club 82 was a celebrity and wise-guy hellhole. The Nursery with pool table and Union Jack floor, a jukebox that seemed to only ever play one song ("Ride the White Horse"—ode to heroin). Cave Canem, a former bathhouse, went overnight from gay pool parties to a casino with roulette wheels, blackjack tables, and bowtied croupiers. Body Heat looked like Shaft's living room. Brownies had a year-round Christmas tree—Brownie in fur coat and pimp hat with a girl on each arm. The bar sported a Check Your Weapons at the Bar sign, and patrons obligingly handed over guns and daggers. Sometimes we were lucky enough to catch one of the few remaining Checker cabs home.

I moved here—the Lower East Side. Loisaida. The language of the streets was predominantly Spanish—the original European Jewish inhabitants having moved away and the islanders, mainly Puerto Rican, having moved in. People lived out in the street in the sweltering summers: kids cooling off in the torrent of an open hydrant, baseball games at night glowing on televisions run with pirated electricity from lampposts, cards or dominos being played on folding tables, friends and families drinking rum and eating empanadas cooked street-side.

The city was all color and personality, unpredictability and, yes, some peril. There were terrible street battles and gunfights, and people died. Too often the sidewalks wore the spontaneous memorials of botanica candles, flowers, and toys, often followed by a commissioned mural portrait of the overdosed or murdered.

Drug dealers worked the streets openly, lining the junkies up against a wall for hours, then chasing them up the stairs to finish their transaction. Or a bucket dangled on a string from floors above, carrying up the crumpled bills (no change accepted) and dropping down the nickel or dime bags. I learned to carry mugging money in a pocket (hiding the rest in a shoe) and walked home with a key poking out of my fist in case I had to fight.

Our neighborhood was neglected, dirty, and often dangerous, but the streets were pure music and color—salsa and merengue throbbed from cruising cars and speakers in apartment windows, the graffiti murals of Chico and Lee and others glowed like jewels on the walls of abandoned buildings and handball courts. Keith Haring's joyful looping figures, radiant babies, dancing dogs, and political slogans ran the lengths of schoolyards and highway barricades—"Crack is Wack!" "Fight AIDS!" "Free South Africa!" (New York wearing its heart on its sleeve). Jean-Michel Basquiat's SAMO (Same Old Shit) tags and cryptic sayings (now relics in the wake of his gallery career) ran along the bricks; Richard Hambleton's spatter figures skulked eerily in corners. We saw Keith at the nightclubs, Jean-Michel riding his bike through the park, Richard hobbling or nodding out at his gas station turned art space, fenced with the metal sculptural madness of the Rivington Street welders, fifteen feet high and topped with the chassis of an old car.

Iggy Pop lived on Avenue B., Philip Glass on Second Avenue. On Fourth Street were the dreadlocked punk rockers Bad Brains and purple-haired octogenarian Quentin Crisp. Penny Arcade at P.S. 122. Ethyl Eichelberger, Wendy Wild, and the drag queens at the Pyramid. Jim Jarmusch and Richard Hell strolled the East Village streets, and Rockets Redglare hauled his massive wrecked frame through the bars. Allen Ginsberg was everywhere—poetry readings, protests, squatter fundraisers.

On summer weekends, there would be Puerto Rican parties down by the East River—music pumping, people dancing, stalls selling all kinds of island foods and rum drinks, T-shirts and trinkets for sale, dominoes and gambling, even prize wheels whirling in percussion. Everyone was welcome.

We lived paint spattered and plaster dusted, hauling canvases and wood, tools and metals to loft work spaces or minuscule apartments, coloring the streets with spray paint and stencils, wheat-pasted posters and scrawled bon mots. We found our furniture on the street. We were artists and poets, writers and musicians, punks and junkies.

I was one of the squatters—a loose coalition of a few hundred people both new to and of the neighborhood—who moved into many of the abandoned buildings of this devastated area, using found and recycled materials to repair roofs and raise floors, teaching each other skills, and creating homes out of the neglect and rubble of the city's cast-off housing stock. We fixed roofs, raised sagging floors, ran plumbing and electrical wiring, carving homes out of shells. We had art shows and performances at Bullet Space—my home—which ran a screen-printing facility and gallery and had a stage in the backyard that hosted everything from musicians, dancers, and poets to fire-eaters, theater, and radical puppet shows. C-Squat threw punk-rock shows and built a half-pipe in the basement for skateboarders. Umbrella house had a printing press for artists, activists, and comic books. We had constantly changing murals and artwork on our building fronts—bursts of color and political outbursts. We fought police evictions on the streets and the city in court and eventually won the right to keep our buildings.

We worked with our neighbors and planted community gardens after clearing abandoned, rubble strewn lots. Some lots hosted casitas, little houses built by Puerto Ricans and other island transplants to bring a little country to their city. Ducks, chickens, and rabbits lived there. A rooster woke me way too early every day for a year.

So much has changed—and where is my beloved city? The East Village, like the rest of the city (but at a more furious pace), has groaned under an onslaught of development—the demolitions and bulldozers, wrecking balls and pile drivers fueling construction of so many expensive apartment buildings, the rents insanely high even by city standards. It is now more expensive to buy real estate in the East Village than on Madison Avenue. Tiny dark spaces in the older buildings are "renovated" and equally pricey. Longtime residents are forced out and away—to where? I have friends born in this neighborhood who can no longer afford to live here.

SoHo, once a symbol of an art and artists' community, has simply become the ultimate monster of gentrification. The artists long gone, even the early gentrifying galleries have fled to Chelsea, priced out by the Gaps and Guccis, Old Navys, and Duane Reeds. This quirky nickname for the area south of Houston Street has only led to a real estate fury to give every neighborhood catchy and, now sadly, generic monikers. NoHo (north of Houston), NoLIta (north of Little Italy),

TriBeCa (triangle below Canal), NoCa (north of Canal), NoMad (north of Madison Park), BoHo (Bowery and Houston)—should be HoBo!

The East Village (now a very expensive and trendy destination for models and stockbrokers) is described as being anywhere from Broadway below Fourteenth Street across to Avenue D (Alphabet City having too many dangerous connotations of a non-white or non-moneyed type). The gorgeous red bricks of the old tenement houses are ripped out and replaced by instant prefab apartment buildings. The bodegas and *cuchifrito* counters are being usurped by upscale restaurants, four-dollar lattes, and "quirky" gift shops. The famous shopping district of Orchard Street exists only on historic signposts, its storefronts now so many trendy bars and bistros, frat party central on weekends.

The fire of Hell's Kitchen is dimmed and advertised as Midtown West or Clinton. The vibrant Dominican community of Washington Heights is disguised in real estate listings as Hudson Heights. My friend calls her Chelsea neighborhood "the Mall of America"—dominated as it is by massive stores Barnes & Noble, Bed Bath & Beyond, TJ Maxx, Best Buy, Burlington Coat Factory, Staples, and of course McDonalds and Starbucks.

Kmart looms over Astor Place. Two massive Home Depots recently opened in Manhattan, offering priority hiring to employees of the city's hardware stores they are putting out of business.

This development and gentrification comes on the heels of the city's "quality of life" programs and hardline policing strategies, mainly under former Mayors Koch and Giuliani. The city is a safer place—but for whom? And at what price? The brutal reality of gentrification is spelled out in evictions, lost jobs, the elimination of cheap housing.

The eviction of eighty-nine-year-old grandmother Eleanor Bumpurs in 1984 ended with her shotgunned to death by police. A 1985 antigraffiti arrest left twenty-two-year-old Michael Stewart choked to death in a Fourteenth Street subway station, for supposedly writing on a wall with a felt-tip marker. In the 1990s, Giuliani's Street Crimes Unit, in the name of getting guns off the streets, led an undercover "stop-and-frisk" action aimed at minority males walking the streets of their own neighborhoods. Thousands were targeted. My friend's son, a schoolboy in Harlem during this time, was so traumatized by the constant abuse he suffered from the police that he refuses to return to the city.

Undercover cops in the Bronx shot unarmed African immigrant Amadou Diallo, a man I knew, forty-one times in the doorway of his home. Teenager Timothy Stansbury was shot to death by a cop while crossing the roof of his Brooklyn building with CDs for a party. My friend's landlord went to jail in 1998 for hiring a hitman to kill her neighbor living in a rent-controlled apartment with a drug overdose.

And the city's willingness to be landlord enforcer came to a furious head the same year when the eviction of squatters in three buildings on East Thirteenth Street was carried out with hundreds of riot cops, a days-long shutdown of the block, and the charge of the NYPD's armored vehicle—a tank!—against the residents and families who had lived in these buildings for up to twenty years. Police sharpshooters stormed through neighboring apartment buildings to take up positions on the rooftops, and the media were corraled behind the wire fence of an empty lot (the only outrage the television stations reported). Giuliani's city going to war on its own people.

The parks now have midnight curfews and fences to keep you off the grass. Barricades herd pedestrians in Midtown. The Barnes & Noble "superstores" have eliminated so many beloved independent bookstores. There are over 150 Starbucks cafes in Manhattan alone, gobbling up the unique and independent coffee houses of city lore.

The resurrected cabaret law (actually created in the 1920s to prevent whites and blacks from dancing together in Harlem nightclubs) is now being used as a revenue-raising bludgeon that bans dancing without a license! My friend's club was padlocked because the bartender was dancing (again). You cannot legally smoke in a bar.

Cops ticket beer drinkers on working-class Rockaway Beach but not the wine drinkers picnicking at the Philharmonic concerts in Central Park. Mayor Bloomberg defended this logic saying the park crowds are better behaved.

The Bowery, for all of New York's history a place for the dispossessed and alone, the itinerant men with nowhere else to go, has lost all but two of its hotels and charity houses to restaurants and luxury buildings. Multimillion-dollar lofts tower over the street. Next to the last men's home, the 125-year-old stained-glassed Bowery Mission, is a velvet-roped nightclub called Mission! A new luxury apartment building on East Seventh Street opened with its lobby featuring giant photographs of street people!

Cause trumpeting—gloating its result. Insult to injury.

Little Italy's Mulberry Street is now a theme park of shiny restaurants and pastry cafes—the butchers, barbershops, and bakeries of real life now supremely expensive boutiques and trendy eateries.

Times Square is Disneyland.

Harlem's heart as an African American neighborhood is being bought out—investors and stockbrokers are buying up the fabled brownstones. Sugar Hill, pride of the black bourgeoisie from the 1920s, is falling out of black hands, as are so many homes and businesses in the area. One Hundred Twenty-fifth Street is as full of Old Navy, Starbucks, Duane Reade, Body Shop, and VIM sneaker stores as any other shopping block in the city.

The buttons, bows, and trimmings of the notions stores that filled Thirty-seventh and Thirty-eighth streets are now as scarce as the clothing companies and manufacturers that created the fashion district. There's a statue of an old man at a sewing machine and another of a giant button and needle, like bronze tombstones, on Seventh Avenue.

The dozens of restaurant supply stores along Bowery near Houston—selling everything from pizza ovens, refrigeration cases, and barstools to pots and pans, whisks and spoons—are all losing their leases and disappearing. Soon so will the thousands of twinkling chandeliers and lamps of the lighting stores to the south.

The shops of Orchard Street are being leveled in huge swaths for boutique hotels and apartment complexes. And all over the city we are suddenly deluged with banks taking up two and three storefronts and often whole street corners. Banks everywhere.

Chinatown is now full of T-shirt and souvenir shops, although there is still a booming underground economy selling fake designer bags. Fireworks for Chinese New Year—a tradition for thousands of years—are banned. The Indian restaurants of Sixth Street are fewer and farther between as leases expire and new businesses arrive. The fish market has been relocated to the Bronx, abandoning its historic site in the original port of the city. Now the South Street Seaport is a tourist shopping and food mall with cobblestones, a maritime museum, and sailing ships for color. The Meatpacking District has become one of the most expensive housing markets and nightclub- and boutique-saturated areas of the city.

What happens to the elderly, minority, poor, and unemployed working people of these neighborhoods? This is a city geared for profit, not for humanity. Not for workers, but for consumers. In the 1980s, Mayor Koch famously, and presciently, said, "If you can't afford to live here—move!"

The East Village used to be the place where the artists and writers, the misfits and weirdos could come to live and make a community. Creativity and possibility were everywhere. Now it is the playground of identically styled college girls and boys with Gap clothes and perfectly blonded hair. The neighborhood embraces them with sports bars, general store–themed restaurants, and Starbucks cafes. And their parents pay the rent.

I still adore New York. It's the most creative place in the world. And we have our victories. The squatters who worked and fought so hard for their homes will soon own their remaining eleven buildings as limited equity co-ops. A creative coalition of gardeners, activists, and their neighbors (and a quarter-million dollar gift from Bette Midler) channeled the outrage of a city and defeated Giuliani's plan to sell off all the community gardens in the five boroughs. They secured hundreds of these gardens forever. And thank goodness the outer boroughs continue the tradition of the famed melting pot of immigrants of ethnic, religious, and racial diversity. Our streets, every day, are a glorious mix of people from all over the world. Artists, moving outward, are founding new communities in Brooklyn and the Bronx.

Change is inevitable—it is how the city lives and breathes. And I don't begrudge a safer neighborhood—no one wants to dodge bullets or have to fight off a mugger with a two-by-four or a kitchen knife or a gun (as I did). But I do know that the city is suffering a terrible loss. Vibrant and distinct communities, neighborhoods, and personalities are leaving the city. I feel sad and angry that the only newcomers to Manhattan from now on will be those rich enough to buy their way in. No new immigrants will bring their ways and flavors and styles to our neighborhoods. No poor artists or writers or musicians will come here and fight to prove their worth. No struggle, no adventure—just pay to stay.

A city that spoke its stories so vividly from its sidewalks and street corners, in its red brick walls and brownstones, is being swiftly and irretrievably mortared over, cleaned off, and dressed up in prefab, becoming a generic wash punctuated by chain stores and tourist destinations. And the immensely rich history that this city wore so proudly and loudly on its streets and in its different neighborhoods is disappearing under a bland layer of gentility, servility, and newly moneyed gloss. New York will be recognizable only by its landmarks, not in its vibrant and historic mix.

I miss the openness and unpredictability of the city. The different music and languages floating in the air. I miss the creativity in the clubs, the art on the streets, the intensity of distinct neighborhoods. I miss the mayhem.

ARE HIGH. A SURGE
WAY
W 42 ST
NEW 42 ST
7 AV
THE WB PRESENTS
Related
MONDAYS 9PM
WB 11
Spanky's
BBQ

SUBURBAN MANHATTAN

Neil Smith and Deborah Cowen

Between 1988 and 1995, the national and international press carried periodic images of riot police with batons, shields, and half-track tanks, rousting homeless people from Tompkins Square Park in New York's Lower East Side or evicting squatters who had made their homes in buildings abandoned by the city's real estate capitalists. Today's portraits of New York City, by contrast, are more likely to highlight Disney's remake of Times Square, SoHo's fashion chic, a new renaissance in Harlem, or the bar and restaurant scene downtown. Neighborhoods such as the Lower East Side and Brooklyn's Williamsburg have long since passed from edgy frontier fascination into advertising text and image in the *New York Times* or MTV. The very wealthy center still rules, as the unseemly corporate struggle over Ground Zero attests, but it is a center increasingly recolonized by the money and mores of the suburban classes whose parents abandoned the postwar city and by wealthy professional migrants attracted by the center's verve. In barely two decades, gentrification and immigration have turned New York City inside out.

The gentrification of New York is no longer about doing up a cute three-story flat or brownstone in the Village or Park Slope, no longer simply about getting a bit of the urban. Today's gentrification is about full-spectrum real estate dominance. Nothing is not in play. Gentrification no longer slinks around a reluctant infrastructure or poses itself, Jane Jacobs style, as a reincarnation of the past, an antidote to the modern. Gentrification *is* the modern, *is* the future, *is* the infrastructure. Highways, amusement parks, malls, megadevelopments—the kinds of infrastructure long associated with suburbs—have gone from being the antithesis of gentrification to its most vital anchors.

The recent redevelopment of Times Square has transformed this former symbol of squalid, dystopic urbanism into a playground for tourists.

The Gates public art project in February 2005 by Christo and Jeanne-Claude may seem like the most urban of all possible public art events. Its venue after all was that most urban of spaces: Central Park. But a simple gestalt switch renders its suburbanism as vivid as the trail of orange banners that were visible to air travelers descending on the city. Seventy-five hundred steel-and-PVC gates, sixteen feet high, hung with nylon (their color gentrified, in official descriptions, as "saffron"), were installed around the walkways of Central Park with most concentrated at the park's south end. When *The Gates* project was first proposed in 1979, it was rejected out of hand in the city council; it was simply too weird and frivolous for a city with high unemployment, a fiscal crisis hangover, and a suburban-living elite of bankers and developers intent on grabbing power back from city residents and politicians. A quarter century later, however, the administration of billionaire Michael Bloomberg championed the project that cost an estimated $21 million. The artists absorbed the costs, more than recouping their outlay by selling drawings for the project and related kitsch. Mayor Bloomberg himself bought two such drawings at a reported price of $800,000, and the future market for these objets d'art will ensure a significant profit.

It was an extraordinary event. Four million people strolled through the installation in just sixteen days, with an estimated 300,000 people coming from London, Sydney, Tokyo, and other corners of the world to see this global media "happening." *The Gates* was embraced above all by the suburbs: upper-middle-class empty nesters, who vigorously avoided visiting their offspring in the city, dropped all squeamishness and rushed in; New Jerseyites and Long Islanders crammed the trains and tunnels to be part of it; retired Connecticut couples used the occasion to spend a few weeks "doing" the city's art scene. Around the park, wealthy condo owners held lavish parties to survey the landscape, or else they rented out their park-view apartments for thousands of dollars for two-hour afternoon "*Gates* parties."

Opinions about the artistic worthiness of *The Gates* were sharply divided. For every visitor who found it an excuse for an unaccustomed contemplative walk through the leaf-bare and sometimes snow-covered park, or a celebration for community togetherness in a city still said (however dubiously) to be hurting after 9/11, others were far less accepting. For many it was a nonevent with no necessary meaning, the perfect Seinfeldian spoof for the city that produced the famous sitcom "about nothing." Seinfeld worked precisely by urbanizing the escapist narcissism of the suburbs, which was such a burbling motif of 1960s sociology; Christo and Jeanne-Claude delivered Central Park. *The Gates* succeeds "precisely by being...a big nothing," writes Peter Schjeldahl in the *New Yorker*. It "lets us get right down to being crazy about ourselves, in a bubble of participatory narcissism." Elsewhere, the *New York Times* lamented the transformation of the "metropolitan oasis" of Central Park into "a psychedelic drive-through car wash." Art as sitcom car-wash takes the city by storm.

Nor was this accidental. For Bloomberg, "it showed the world that New York is safe and exciting"—the suburbs with pizzazz?—but *The Gates* also brought an additional $254 million in tourist spending to the city in a month of traditionally weak tourism. Art has long been a vehicle for projecting a safe, gentrified persona for the new hygienic urbanism, even when in the 1980s, it was the raw grunginess of much Lower East Side art (itself often antagonistic to gentrification) that paradoxically carried this responsibility. But the rawer art of that period quickly diffused outward to Brooklyn and Jersey City, routed by the very gentrification it helped spawn. The earlier street art energy of the 1970s was likewise bleached from the sides of subway cars and dissipated into the commodified gallery spaces of the 1990s. Today a new graffiti art project on Houston Street is sponsored by Time Inc. While the "slum arts" of the 1970s and 1980s projected city neighborhoods outward, *The Gates* turns this art history inside out, sanitizing the city's image from the global inward. In an ironic twist, on the installation's final day, it was the subject of a suburban prank. Wandering through the park a half hour after its 1 a.m. curfew, three youths used magic markers to write graffiti, including their names, on four of the gates. This was no case of urban revenge against invaders; the perpetrators, who had already been ticketed for breaking the curfew, were traced to their homes in suburban New Jersey and subsequently charged with criminal mischief.

Manhattan Mall was opened in 1989 near the crossroads of Broadway, Sixth Avenue, and Thirty-fourth Street, right in the middle of Midtown. It was a provocation to many New Yorkers, the invasion of the city snatchers. Just across the street from the venerable Macy's—the epitome of New York urban shopping (itself long since suburbanized with branches across the country's crabgrass frontier from Bloomington to Pasadena and in Springfields everywhere from Ohio to New Jersey)—Manhattan Mall was greeted by sniffs of antisuburban snobbery. The business concept behind the project held that the city had to emulate the suburbs that were increasingly winning the war for retail dollars. It was hardly a new idea, but it became New York's planning mantra by the 1990s: the city had to emulate the suburbs to survive. Middle-class suburbs were built to have everything private, protected, and accessible, if not always close, and Manhattan Mall replicated the model with corporate power, private security, and a location where several subway lines converge. It boasted eight stories of retail space with all the usual mall denizens—Sam Goody, Victoria's Secret, Strawberry, Bath and Body Works, Brookstone—and a ninth-story "food court" with Midtown views. "Consumers who want an orderly shopping environment where they can bring families on the weekend, commuters, and tourists," say the owners, "will drive sales" at the mall. Sure enough, despite dire predictions of failure, the city's masses flocked to Manhattan Mall as much as they circulate every weekend in the suburbs.

It was not the first and it was far from the last mall in Manhattan. When the Trump Mall opened on Fifth Avenue several years earlier, it was seen as too idiosyncratic to connote anything other than the extravagant ego of its eponymous developer. But malls, once the quintessential anti-New York of suburban culture, now dot the city's landscape from Harlem USA to the Shops at Columbus Circle to Chinatown's East Broadway Mall. The only difference between Manhattan and the suburbs is that the city malls are more vertical than horizontal, and locational success within the mall is less geared to centrality than to height. The urban mall reverses the traditional gradient in rent and prestige that increases with elevation: in the mall, the lower street-level floors command the highest rent, and the higher floors are more likely to lie vacant. But even this difference is collapsing. Thirty-fourth Street between Fifth and Seventh avenues is a mall of name-brand stores that lacks only a single roof; Broadway in SoHo is much the same. New York's malls even span the same range of styles and clientele, from the twee of Short Hills (Trump Mall) to the bland functionality of Anywhere USA (Manhattan Mall). Box stores such as Home Depot and Best Buy, which long circled the city with menacing suburban intent, have now invaded Manhattan, while Target has set up in Brooklyn.

With the Walt Disney Company as its centerpiece, Times Square is Manhattan's roofless mall par excellence. From Southern California to Central Florida, Disney had for decades reconstructed Main Street as suburban simulacra, as long as it was far from the chaotic frisson of real city streets. The Disney Company during the Cold War epitomized the anticity of American popular culture, even or especially when its movies happened in cities. What would it do with America's real main street—Forty-second Street—which by the 1980s had come to symbolize a squalid dystopic urbanism? One Disney plan was to gate the whole neighborhood—a kind of Truman Show social bubble without the dome (not coincidentally, the new urbanist architects of Seaside, Florida, where the movie *The Truman Show* was shot also participated in building the Disney-sponsored town, Celebration). A less drastic piece of Disney imagineering, equally intended to ensure Disney's trademark of total locational control, would have monopolized all of Forty-second Street by implanting Disney businesses in all its shopfronts. Despite such grander ambitions, and after hardscrabble power politics, the company eventually scaled back to a single large Disney Store. Mickey Mouse moved in where XXX sex stores, now banished to postindustrial Queens, had once filled the interstices between Broadway theaters.

In the spectacle of Times Square, flash conquers fact. Electronic adverts stretching up skyscraper wallfronts boost the world's commodities to ambulant consumers below—Kodak and McDonald's, Nike and Nissan—but Times Square has moved on from the emblematic Camel Man, blowing smoke into the air. In a cacophony of screaming yet soundless images, electronic jumbotrons weave and bob with the restlessness of video-age kids' attention spans or the suburban driving patterns of their parents shuttling them from activity to activity. Repetition and unpredictability cascade into the "crossroads of the world" like high-speed journeys on known but never knowable trajectories: movies (*Lion King*, *Star Wars*), electronics (iPod), plays (*Fiddler on the Roof*), financial companies (Ernst & Young), the stock market. NASDAQ's jumbotron is the most expensive ever, costing $2 million in annual rent.

In New York, where shopping is a sport, what could be more natural than a spectacular makeover led by a company that pioneers "retail as entertainment." All the more fitting is that this remake has focused on the entertainment district of Broadway. The city wagered that a Disney anchor store would attract other brand name businesses. Whether Disney was the catalyst or not, brand names flooded in as tenants or advertisers. Toys "R" Us and Gap joined corporate chains (Europa Cafe, Starbucks), entertainment companies (MSNBC, MTV, ABC), and office travel and news companies (Reuters, Condé Nast) in an area already named for the *New York Times*.

Incongruent urbanisms certainly intervene—a military recruitment station and an NYPD storefront of *Law and Order* fame. In 2004 a curious U.S. Drug Enforcement Agency exhibit (and shop) appeared next door to the Disney Store, and with $1.5 million of taxpayer money it hosted a Target America exhibit that warned anyone who wandered in that "drugs fund terrorism." (No mention is made of the Reagan government's Iran-Contra sponsorship of drug-dealing Contra terrorists in Nicaragua or of CIA-sponsored drug distribution in California in the same period.) The exhibit decamped for a Midwest tour in 2005.

Ten years before *The Gates*, as Disney was concluding negotiations over the transformation of Times Square, the company used its political and economic power to privatize Central Park for a day. Mayor Giuliani rented the park to Disney, which after nine months of planning fenced off the park's Great Lawn, converted it into a giant screening room, provided VIP box seats, and on four giant eighty-foot screens proceeded to launch its blockbuster animation movie *Pocahontas*. A mammoth urban drive-in, it was the largest film premiere in history. The electricity consumed was equal to that used to power the World Trade Center during the event, and the public without tickets was excluded. Disney has made a business of trumping while controlling the public in the cultural mastery of the suburban space, and they now managed it in Manhattan. By contrast—or perhaps in the same vein—Mayor Bloomberg refused to grant public access to the park for a resolutely noncorporate event when the 2004 Republican National Convulsion (as it was popularly known in New York) was in town. Protestors wanted to demonstrate in the park against the Iraq war and Bush's election, but they were persistently denied a permit. Mayor Bloomberg, meanwhile, to make the prohibition seem democratic, initiated rules that prevent more than 50,000 people from attending any single event on the Great Lawn and limit the number of such events to six per year. The crowd size, location, and number of events are judiciously chosen to allow New York's Opera in the Park and Shakespeare in the Park to fill the existing slots while other events are effectively barred. Whether Disney has the political or economic clout to be granted a future exception, unlike antiwar protestors, remains to be seen.

The Theater District is more clearly in focus from the suburbs, which provide the vast majority of its audience, than it is from a city that already lives as a spectacle and does not need or even want that spectacle played back through the lenses of avaricious corporate glitz. Always of the suburbs, Broadway is now more than ever a tourist outpost on Manhattan Island. Times Square imagery, quite unlike the people in the street, is dense with suburban-clean white middle-class faces and bodies, with the odd "exotic" mixed in; its allure of commodities to be wolfed down by the weekly paycheck, the sick connection between macho sports bravado and the fantastic availability of women's bodies poured from a bottle. Sex sells, of course, and the nexus between gender, sex, and sport dominates Times Square. ESPN Zone flashes alongside Budweiser, a major sports advertiser, presenting Barbie women for testosterone-charged men watching football; the New York Yankees gaze out toward scantily clad women advertising just about everything.

Sex and the City became a blockbuster hit as the new Times Square was unfolding. It was produced by HBO (a major Disney competitor), which also muscled a broadcasting studio into Times Square. Had the sitcom been made three decades earlier, it would have been called *Sex and the Suburbs*. This was the era of swingers, key parties, and so-called wife swapping, an era capped by the Hollywood effort *Bob, Carol, Ted and Alice*, and revisited more recently in Ang Lee's study of suburban sexual "revolution" in *Ice Storm*. Of course in the 1960s and 1970s, sex on TV was much more controlled, but away from the cameras it nonetheless became the focus of intense psychological and sociological research by scholars bent on rejecting the stereotype of staid suburban Babbittry. The suburbs were always gendered, of course, the legendary domain of the wife-mother-consumer running the postwar nuclear family in the absence of the commuting father, but all that has changed. Most women today work outside the home, and fewer commuters do the suburb-to-city shuffle. The suburbs never were their stereotype, but they have also changed into far more functionally (if not socially) integrated places. Edge cities mix suburb with city, and gentrified cities do the same. In *Sex and the City*, sex becomes a sport—much as it was for many in 1970s suburbia—but it is a sport played primarily by sexy women, which guarantees a cross-gender audience. Where better than the city to get a sense of the romance and danger that sporting sex brings? The Women's Entertainment channel has its own jumbotron in Times Square. Just like *Seinfeld*, *Sex and the City* urbanizes recognizably suburban fantasies of city life, independence, and narcissism.

Incongruent urbanisms crash into congruent suburbanism. Or do they? Just a few yards from the NYPD storefront in Times Square and from the famed U.S. military recruiting post favored as the target for antiwar demonstrations, HBO, releasing its hit *Oz* as a DVD, redid a Times Square building to replicate a walled prison. *Oz* was a "real-life" prison drama, and HBO simulated a barbed-wire fence around a stone prison to create for visitors the feel of a city under siege by city recidivists. The suburbs have long been about security—economic, physical, environmental, racial—and a city that did not emulate the ontological security of the suburbs could not compete. Times Square's success lies precisely in knitting a hint of urban danger ("we're not in the suburbs anymore, Toto") into the suburban fetish for security. It serves up city-dangerous as suburban-safe and commodifies it to boot. A suburban fantasy on steroids. Getting a bit of the city with · a return train ticket in your pocket.

The Times Square remake strongly suggests that the suburbanization of New York City has everything to do with capitalizing real estate that was long left in the loss column. No major real estate developer was left behind when the call was made to the trough of $1.5 billion of taxpayer subsidies that lubricated the project. Some of the most unseemly struggles pitted these developers against each other and the city. But a quieter yet more pervasive suburbanization of New York is happening through the same powerful economic actors in the less-glitzy neighborhoods where gentrification does not bring people back from the suburbs but where, rather, the suburbs donate their younger generation who choose not to leave. The Lower East Side does not yet have suburban malls, but it will. They do not yet have Disney, but they have global finance, suburban developers, and international landlords. The defeat of the homeless/squatters/neighborhood/activist struggles in the early 1990s opened the neighborhood up to a transformation that has become permanent. Williamsburg was next on the Pac-man suburban munching of the city—Harlem, Astoria, "lower" Park Slope,

Jersey City, Bushwick, Bed-Stuy, Sunset Park—it's no longer a Manhattan story. Neighborhoods where desperate renters follow the outward disinvestment of owners and landlords become the new urban fantasy for real estate professionals and apartment hunters alike. Tenants' rents pay for a reinvestment that simply expands the gentrification frontier, chasing the receding suburbs that accelerate away from people's dreams and evict them in the process. Yet the suburbs are also changing, becoming the city, rushing back in, leapfrogging the world of the city's working class, immigrants, bad housing. In the middle they meet: gentrification becomes suburbanization while it also chases the suburban dream to its edges—bumping up against the newly urbanizing edge cities. The suburbs urbanize as the city suburbanizes. Is this where urban grunge gives way to suburban chic while suburban grunge becomes corporatized urban chic?

NEWS FROM NOWHERESVILLE

Time Warner's "Center of Everything" Comes to New York

Eric Darton

Whither New York? Wither New York? You don't know. You never can second-guess this place for all the years you've lived here—fifty-five and counting. What you do know is that there is no one narrative the city tells itself that cannot be countered by another one just as urgent, just as seemingly emblematic of the whole organism's bedrock state of being. But then, in a New York minute—an eye blink—the present all-encompassing story is superseded by another, so confident of its own totality that even people with good memories lose hold of the moment that came before.

On top of which, this city, like any high-pressure mixing chamber, is a won-der house of parallel coincident universes. Bounding up those subway steps, a thuggy-looking guy pauses to ask a women struggling with a stroller, shopping bags hanging off the handles, if she needs a hand. They don't know one another from Adam and Eve, but she nods, decoding his gesture, not his language, be-cause they were both born in entirely different parts of the world. Together, they make a swift and fast-adhering bond of trust that lasts exactly as long as it takes to emerge onto the street, set the stroller down, and go their separate ways.

It's afternoon now. Later tonight, a young man you recall seeing around the neighborhood, though he lives in the Bronx, will shoot another young man to death in an elevator over a scarcity of drug turf. The shooter, aged eighteen, is the father of one child. The shootee—around the same age—leaves behind four kids. You won't find out about what happened until tomorrow morning, but tonight the

Looking west along Central Park South (Fifty-ninth Street) toward the twin towers of the Time Warner Center at Columbus Circle. The shopping center on its lower floors imitates an upscale suburban shopping mall, something heretofore unknown in Manhattan.

police choppers flying low over the neighborhood, their spotlights blazing, will signal as clearly as any bush telegraph that someone died badly in the projects.

This New York feels eternal, a small gesture of connection eclipsed by the dreadful news of a life cut short. Such events rearrange the atmosphere for a nanosecond, and then the urban Leviathan sucks them up and moves on. Fleeting blips in the collective awareness, they neither change the face of the city nor signify some bone-deep shift in the economics, the culture—the cumulative story the city tells itself about what it has become. What is seismic enough to do that? What hits the body of such a big and complex organism with enough force to get its attention, shake it out of one mode of being and into another? What lets the city know its balance has definitively shifted?

The signifiers used to arrive in far more grandiose and explicit packages. Is it possible to imagine alterations to the cityscape and its consciousness at the level of Central Park, the Brooklyn Bridge, or the Empire State Building? We haven't had a megaproject like the Cross Bronx Expressway or the World Trade Center for well over a generation now. In the recent past, the closest thing New York has experienced to an upbuilding event that truly shifted the pulses is the Time Warner Center. How would one quantify its effect in ballistic terms? Say the cumulative firepower of two thousand Starbucks? You don't get many interventions like this in one lifetime. Hopefully.

A "mutha" of an intersection is Columbus Circle, strategically placed at the lower left-hand corner of Central Park. Here Fifty-ninth Street is skewered at an odd angle by Broadway and at ninety degrees by Eighth Avenue—the latter turns to Central Park West on the north side. That huge building at the southwest arc of the circle? That's the Time Warner Center, built on the spot where Robert Moses's Coliseum used to stand. You watched them pull the old building down, by inches really. What did it take, six months, a year, to achieve level ground? Like Moses himself, the Coliseum didn't go quietly. Its prestressed concrete hung together, clung to the steelwork like something out of Albert Speer's Berlin game—built to last the lifespan of a Thousand Year Reich. And if not that, then at least present a worthy piece of "ruin value" in its premature destruction.

Great pneumatic hammers banged at the Coliseum's supports and shuddered on the rebound. You can only imagine what sort of havoc the pounding did to the kidneys of the machine operators. Bulldozers clambered up the great mound of rubble then disappeared over the crest and down the other side. Generations of wheat-pasted advertisements shredded off the plywood perimeter once bravely stenciled Post No Bills. For the longest time it felt as if the ordeal of this awful building would never end. And now the Coliseum is gone, and this, this incommensurable thing, stands its stead.

How did the Time Warner Center get here? The story is a long one, and boring really, offering nothing of the titanic power politics, none of the heartbreaking displacements, the traumatic super blocking of an old low-rise district that attended the World Trade Center's coming thirty-five years before. Altogether absent too is any sense that, at the turn of the millennium, the city was passing through a threshold transposing its very nature into another key and, via a dramatic augmentation of its skyline, entering another epoch. In New York, as throughout much of the Western world, the notion of progress had been superseded by the free-floating, disengaged assumption that "shit happens." In the time span between the building of the World Trade and Time Warner centers, all pretenses of planning in the interest of a wider public good, however compromised, had given way to a scramble for who could get away with what and make it stick. The new race of city shapers had moved beyond paternalism, beyond the brutality of the urban renewal ethos, into a kind of glossy globalist anomie in which greed was blandly accepted as the prime underlying motive behind all human acts.

Succinctly put, what happened at the Columbus Circle crossroads was this: in the early 1950s, Moses took title to the future Coliseum site via the eminent domain powers of his Triborough Bridge and Tunnel Authority. He knocked down a couple of venerable landmarks, the Colonnade Building and Park Theatre, and raised the Coliseum, topped by a twenty-five-story office block. Conceived as a kind of concrete tent for trade fairs, the Coliseum, poorly designed as an exposition space, was already obsolete the day it opened in 1956. When, in the mid-1980s, the vast and mall-like Javits Convention Center sprawled out on the far West Side south of Thirty-fourth Street, the fate of Moses's dodo was sealed. At some point after the Power Broker was stripped of his agencies in the early 1970s, the ceaseless trade-offs among political and financial machers on the boards of public corporations landed the Coliseum in the lap of the Metropolitan Transit Authority (MTA).

What followed were several rounds of Request for Proposals (RFPs), a dozen years of inconclusive angling by every conceivable real estate biggie, and much ado about the shadow the vast structures envisioned would cast across the park. Then one day in the late 1990s, whamo!—the deal went down. A suitably obscure entity called Columbus Center presided over the slapdash and fatality-marred demolition of the Coliseum, and The Related Co.—related to what and to whom?—won the bid as lead partner in developing a mixed-use, twin-towered complex that would trumpet, in honor of the latest media mega-merger, AOL TIME WARNER CENTER in big silvery letters across its broad marquee. Anyone who questioned what the MTA, whose job it is to run the subway and bus lines, was doing in the real estate business, or otherwise yelled "we wuz robbed!"—by virtue of an enormous piece of public property being privatized without benefit of the citizenry's say-so—was drowned out in the clang of steel on steel, the rumble of ready-mix trucks, and the sluicing sound of concrete pouring down the chutes.

You cannot claim to have gone out of your way to record the Time Warner Center's progress—it seemed, after all, like another stultifying variation on the timeworn theme of Grab Land to Build Towers—but you did take notice when your path crossed Columbus Circle and sometimes took notes as well. And gradually it dawned on you that the monster they were raising up constituted a beast of a new order in the city's evolution—a vertical mall in which architectural overkill and conspicuous consumption would intertwine more potently than the city had ever witnessed, or absorbed, before. When you page through your journal today, you read what you saw unfolding then.

✶ ✶ ✶

January 20, 2002 Up at Columbus Circle, snowcapped, its steelwork shrouded, New York's newest twin-towered folly riseth apace. The name "Time Warner" itself sounds like a B-movie victim's dying gasp: "No time—warn her!" And what to make of the acronym AOL? Absence Of Liberty. Almost Outta Luck. Here comes the AOL Time Warner Center like a bat out of hell, someone gets in our way, someone doesn't feel so well—a creature that, like the World Trade Center once did, projects plenty of aggression but knows no hint of playfulness or irony.

Yet these towers appear less as direct descendants of the trade center than as a bizarre mutation of the older race of residential buildings whose forms came to define the silhouette of Central Park West after World War I: The San Remo, The Century, The Majestic, The El Dorado, The Beresford—twin-peaked standard-bearers from the glory days of the ultraswank Manhattan apartment.

If you were to ride an elevator up to the center's topmost I-beam on a clear day, could you see, as Saul Steinberg did for his famous *New Yorker* cover, over the foothill Rockies and all the way to Hollywood?

February 19, 2002 Where the Coliseum once stood, the Time Warner Center rears up, its monstrous, tortured gridwork of beams absolutely dwarfing Columbus stuck up on his column, marooned like a flagpole sitter left over from the 1930s. Behind Columbus's back and set in the awkward wedge of greenery at the south end of the Trump International Hotel and Tower stands a chrome-plated globe, roughly thirty feet in diameter, planted on a pedestal. In this morning's late winter sun, the globe, with its jagged-edged continents overlaying a gridwork of longitudes, resembles nothing so much as a kindergarten project ("OK, kids, we're going to make a model of the world out of tinfoil") gone absurdly out of hand. True, the flashy metal serves to distract the eye but for little more than an instant amid this hodgepodge of urban mixed signals: the gilded, overwrought memorial remembering the Maine; the funky old Huntington Hartford building; traffic islands; radiating arteries; and beckoning parkland. Now, Trump's globe has shrunk still further—it looks no bigger than a cat toy when set against the vast backdrop of the AOL Time Warner Center as the towers extrude from their massive, asymmetrical plinth. Thus dwarfed, the silvery earth seems less a planet than an unhappy moon, knocked out of orbit and isolated in an alien landscape that can never be home.

Across Broadway, the city's latest twins are not billed as anything so modest as the center of world trade. Bold type bannered across the scaffolding announces the coming Center of Everything. Unlike the oddly passive quality of the World Trade Center's aggression, the Everything Towers present all acute angles and fractal edges undergirded by a heavy-duty steel cage—trusses and buttresses abound. No ticky-tacky bar joists hold up slab floor plates—this puppy is massively overbuilt. Though their designers could not have anticipated 9/11, the violent feng shui of the AOL twins fairly taunts passing jetliners to make their day. These $2-billion dollar babies won't just kill planes, they'll castrate 'em.

From within the matrix of steelwork draped with immense American flags, you hear a repetitive infernal clanging. Soon—you don't know when, but it's bound to happen—the anvil chorus will shift location across Eighth Avenue to the very base of the roundabout and modulate from sounds of construction to those of demolition. They'll be taking down the Huntington Hartford building, even now encased in a matrix of scaffolding. Built in the early 1960s as a gallery to house Hartford's collection, then taken over by the city's Department of Cultural Affairs, and now abandoned, Edward Durrell Stone's strange caprice, the oilliest, most endearing slab building ever designed, still holds fast—for now. Bits of its masonry, unattended, free fall into the netting over the scaffolded walkway below. How many more days?

✖ ✖ ✖

You took no note of the date in your journal, but the center officially opened on the evening of February 4, 2004. Cirque de Soleil, Jewel, and Marc Anthony performed for a black-tie crowd of invited dignitaries and luminaries ranging from the Governor himself to Cindy Crawford and Salman Rushdie. But the gala, intended to endow the center with an "only in New York" stamp of legitimacy, couldn't entirely disguise the fact that an elephant had taken over the living room. Beset by media, the developers found themselves protesting that their vast assemblage of stores was not a mall, but rather a "retail complex." One reporter wouldn't play the semantics game and asked several guests: "So is this a mall, or what?" To which, with only slight variations, came the reply: "Sure looks like a mall to me."

The Time Warner Center was not, by any means, the first mall to be built in New York City. But through a combination of massive scale and prime location, it announced that the suburban ethos, long ascendant, had finally breached the core of Manhattan. Nearly a half century after the assault inflicted by the Cross Bronx Expressway, its essential city-busting strategy had at last been achieved. The mall, preeminent symbol of nowheresville, smacked down hard in the town that not long past had been known worldwide, for better or worse, as the ultimate repository of urban values.

The next mention of the Time Warner Center in your journal comes seven months later.

✖ ✖ ✖

September 28, 2004 Suicide by atrium. A man clambers over the railing on the fourth level, works his way out onto the rafters, then plunges from Samsung past Borders, past Williams-Sonoma, and on down. Lands in front of a big fat Botero bronze. A different trajectory would have carried him further, subterranean, down into the Whole Foods dining court.

"It was like a boom," a witness said of the body as it struck. "We thought a bomb went off. Everybody screamed."

More discreet the dropping of AOL from the center's name.

But now the PR spinners have something real to keep them busy. How do you fit death leaps into your definition of "mixed-use"?

November 13, 2004 You've promised to write a piece for a book on the suburbanization of New York. But how to distill a phenomenon so broad and diffuse down to a concrete instance? Then it hits you. What better symbol of the whole shift in the quality of the city's life than the Time Warner Center—apotheosis of the terror-chic mall?

Accordingly, you pick up your wife from her drawing group at the Art Student's League on Fifty-seventh Street and head over to scope out the thing itself—seemingly balanced atop the housing of each revolving door, a huge silver Christmas tree ball. Festive yet threatening. Push and turn. Hope that if the vibrations disturb this unholy bauble, it rolls off onto the head of the guy coming through behind you. Funny—or not so—how this place induces that "I'm all right Jack" kind of thinking. Wheel of fortune. Whew, you're inside.

Down the escalator into Whole Foods. Weirdly postapocalyptic, putting a supermarket and food court underground. You perch on adjacent stools, eat dinner of sorts from clear, plastic take-out containers. Other folk resort to green melmacish bowls the color of hospital basins. Less flimsy than what you've got, but the bowls are so steep-sided, the food must all run together at the bottom. The place is packed—turnover so fast it looks time-lapse. But the curried chicken isn't bad. Look around and see feel-good Calcutta. Finish up your coffee—delicious, but jeez, a buck sixty-two for a cuppa joe that small?

The next move is up and out. Nearly blocking off the hall flanking the atrium, a black Lincoln Aviator squats, its cartoon tire treads spreading just enough on the high-sheened marble floor to give a sense of just how much this grotesquely hypertrophied pile of metal weighs. *Win me!* No need to tie yourself to the mast, this siren can't reach you. Whatever car lust you possess is bound up in that elusive vintage Jaguar. As you squeeze around the Aviator, your wife shakes her head. "Exhibit A," she says. "Why we're in Iraq."

✘ ✘ ✘

Flash forward to today. Spring of 2005. Early afternoon. Push through the revolving doors once again and enter the realm of a conglomerate real estate package that encompasses not only the Time Warner and AOL headquarters but also the Mandarin Oriental Hotel and Jazz at Lincoln Center, a multistage project directed by Wynton Marsalis. Lots of retail too: Borders, Sephora, Samsung, Tag Heure watches, Godiva chocolates to name only a few.

Ride the escalator to level four, as high as you can go without a pass. Above you, a host of corporate offices telescope upward and further still in the direction of the stratosphere, two hundred plus condominium apartments—if that term can be applied to living spaces as large as 5,000 square feet—for the likes of Ricky Martin, Lady Henrietta Spencer Churchill, Wynton Marsalis himself, at least one supermodel, roosting pairs of Hollywood and Broadway producers, and the former wife of a senator from New Jersey whose ex must've been lucky in the market since her pad cost $9 million.

Lean against the atrium railing. Look down and then around you. A young woman in a sort of uniform—black pants and a gray polyester livery-style vest over a beige polo shirt—works her way toward you, polishing the surfaces. Every few paces, she stops to spray blue Windex from a capacious bottle, then gives a desultory wipe with her cloth. As she draws closer, you see she's got blonde hair, doughy cheeks with a sprinkle of acne, and wears golden hoop earrings. You move aside for her, but she goes past where you stood and misses a set of palm prints on the wooden railing too large to be yours. Cursorily, she attends to the Formica-covered base of a sculpture. As she straightens up, you notice the left lace of her running shoe's untied.

Interesting sculpture, now that you come to look at it. A bronze around four feet tall. It's by Archipenko—*Soldat qui marche*, dated 1917. Go figure. What is a dynamic, rough-cast Russian Constructivist figure doing isolated among the well-padded seating areas of a twenty-first-century vertical mall? What has become of the young woman? There she is, wiping the glass of the menu case outside the imposing blue doors of a restaurant named Per Se. When she moves on, you scope out the object of her polishing. Behind the glass lies yesterday's Chef's Tasting Menu. Aha, $175 prix fixe.

You give a thought to discreetly tailing the woman as she cleans, letting her seemingly random trajectory guide you through the warrens of this vast no-wheresville, but instead you gravitate back to the edge of the atrium to watch the circulation of the people across the lobby floor, five stories below. From this height and angle, the folks pushing through the revolving door look like they're spinning 'round in the hopper of a food processor. Miraculously, they emerge on the other side intact. Over on your left now, the young woman lightly buffs the cushions of a banquette. Consciously or not, she moves the cloth in time to the rhythm of Dusty Springfield's "Son of a Preacher Man," which leaks over the PA speakers, just audible above the wash of white noise permeating the atrium.

How, you ask yourself yet again, did this monstrous place come to be? Here real estate pornography has been amped up to what must be a kind of ultimate pitch—and along with it every sort of lifestyle porn—except, of course, the honest kind. Words fail. The evil of banality. Every formulation sounds trite. Which is why you keep turning away from the interior and toward the light streaming in from outside through the 250-odd panes of glass—each one perhaps 4 feet by 8—that gridded together make up a single tremendous window facing east. Through this vitreous frame, the intense early green of Central Park unfolds beyond the Merchant's Gate. And a perspective, nothing short of majestic, leads the eye down Fifty-ninth Street along its varicolored stream of horse carriages.

Jaw-dropping in its height, breadth, and clarity, the scene stands as though frozen into a gargantuan CD jewel case. Seemingly just beyond the glass and close enough to touch, Columbus stands atop his pedestal. If he made a quarter turn, you would face one another at eye level. And surrounding him below, a small army of construction workers labors amid heavy machinery and pallets stacked with slabs of cut granite. Some lift mallets to trim the stone, others sweep and shovel—all this human energy bent on remaking the fountain that circles the column on which the Genoese navigator stands.

You tear yourself away and wander along the wing to the atrium's north. The doors stand open so you walk through them and into the V Steakhouse. Beneath your feet, a figured carpet leads to parquet floors. From the lofty ceiling hang a score of chandeliers, ablaze in full daylight, illuminating at every hand the simulated trappings of the Gilded Age. It takes a moment for the maitre d' to approach you during which time you take in, straight ahead through the restaurant's immense windows, the up-close and intimate demolition-in-progress of an ochre brick building, a massive thing, a full block deep and stretching the better part of the distance between Central Park West and Broadway.

What would it feel like to take a spectatorial table, sip a martini, order an appetizer of warm oysters with basil, wasabi, and potato crumbs ($16), and follow it up with the New York State milk-fed veal rib chop ($39)? Over the span of the courses you'd have plenty of time to contemplate the tearing down just beyond the glass, and record in your mind the weathered edge of every punched-out window in the cavernous wreck, each winking plywood patch nailed up here and there as if by some caprice. The whole view, in its way, absent the streaks of arson smoke, echoes the devastated South Bronx of the bad old days.

You settle for the martini, and it's a good one. Not quite at the level of the ones they serve at the Century Club—nothing equals those—but potent enough to separate your head a tad from your body and make you aware of the fascinating optics to be gleaned from the escalator ride downstairs. On the lobby floor stands a shiny burgundy Lincoln Mark LT pickup truck. It is such a Brobdingnagian vehicle that if Botero's bronze woman—fifteen feet tall if she's an inch and half as wide at the hip—were to walk over and open the door, you have a feeling she would find plenty of room inside the cab. In the flatbed of the truck rests a gigantic matching chrome-trimmed motorcycle. Temptation Now Has A Sidekick, runs the banner copy draped along the pickup's side.

Yes, that's it! The moment that ought to happen now. The Botero woman shouldn't stand rooted to her spot, ornamenting this false temple, waiting for the next sacrificial victim to crash down at her feet. What she needs to do is gesture to her man, the other giant bronze gatekeeper who stands twenty feet to her left. They should climb aboard the giant pickup truck and drive off together. Or better yet, forget the Mark LT and just grab the chopper. One on the front seat, the other on the back—gender rules don't apply if you're a sculpture. Just go for it. Crash out through the revolving doors. Once around the circle in triumph they'd go, before heading for the George Washington Bridge. Then straight on—into the soon-to-be sunset and drive all night in the free and open air.

FROM PEDDLERS TO PANINI
The Anatomy of Orchard Street

Amy Zimmer

By the time my great-great-uncle Teddy Eckstein moved from Zelva (a village in what's now Lithuania) to the Lower East Side in 1905, Eastern European Jews already overflowed the narrow tenement-lined cobblestoned streets. Many got their start selling corn, buttons, fish, and anything else they could from pushcarts along Orchard Street before opening up their own wholesale or retail stores. And over the decades, Orchard Street became fixed in the imagination as the city's crowded, chaotic, pulsating hub of low-priced dry goods.

The area still has a powerful nostalgic pull for Jews who fled the Lower East Side with its deteriorating walk-ups for the outer boroughs or Westchester, Long Island, and New Jersey, their place taken by Puerto Ricans, blacks, and Chinese. But over time it devolved from a gritty bargain center into a largely abandoned haven for drugs and prostitution, only to emerge in recent years as a target for speculators anxious to turn this ethnic enclave into another upscale neighborhood. Today the tenements are becoming high-priced condominiums, the dingy stores fashionable bars and boutiques, and the Lower East Side is luring back to the city young professionals. And many of them, me included, are the descendants of immigrants who gave the area its once-vibrant reputation.

At the turn of the twentieth century, Orchard Street was known for dry-goods and handbag stores, while Allen Street shops sold ties. Linens, fabrics, and hosiery were available on Grand Street, ladies' coats were on Division Street, and East Broadway offered fine men's clothes. Teddy was soon joined in this cauldron of commerce by his father, Harris, and brothers Charlie and Meyer, my great-great-grandfather. All four took jobs as salesmen at local dry-goods stores while saving money to open their own. Teddy worked at Kramer Brothers on Canal

With the Eastern European Jewish immigrants hocking wares from pushcarts long gone from Orchard Street and family-owned stores replaced by fashionable shops and restaurants, the remnants of the lost culture of the Lower East Side are now found only at the Tenement Museum where tourists line up prior to embarking on a trip down memory lane.

Street, at that time one of the largest stores with over ninety workers, where he was the top salesman in charge of the hosiery department.

When the family opened H. Eckstein's & Sons in 1916, they initially took a small space on Orchard Street that Teddy ran solo, while the rest of the family continued at their other jobs. But their bosses eventually found out (after all, the Lower East Side merchants were a tight-knit group, and everyone knew everyone else's business) and fired them, forcing the entire clan into Eckstein's full time.

Amid the small townlike neighborhood cohesion, there was a great flurry of competition that spilled out onto the bustling sidewalks. If a customer asked for something a shop was temporarily out of, a salesman would excuse himself and go to the "warehouse." In reality he'd rush to a nearby business and buy the item at cost or at a very low markup just to keep that loyal customer. Adding chaos to the street bazaar of peddlers were salesmen from storefronts "hooking" people inside—sometimes by shouting, sometimes literally by pulling them in. And once customers were inside, storekeepers often didn't let them out without pressuring a sale, a tactic the Ecksteins picked up from their earlier employers. Over time, since Lower East Side prices were always negotiable, they became experts in the art of haggling, and the philosophy never wavered: "Always make the sale!"

No two customers paid the same price for an identical purchase at Eckstein's, yet they almost always received a discount. As soon as shoppers stepped onto the creaky, dusty, wooden floor of that massive store filled with boxes of underwear and hosiery lined up all the way to the corroding tin ceiling, a salesman was peering over at them, asking their names, where they were from, what they wanted to buy, and what they wanted to do with their lives.

Throughout the years, amenities within Eckstein's remained unchanged. Floorboards were broken, poison powder lay in corners to kill off rats, and the chipping green paint in the bathrooms was probably leaden. Instead of an air conditioner in the summer, a large, metal industrial fan would circulate the dusty air. Clothes sat folded on tables, hung in plastic bags, or spilled out of boxes. Sweatshirts and sweaters were near the front door, the men's department was in one corner, children's clothes in another, odds-and-ends and pajamas near the back office. The goods at Eckstein's, including housedresses, work pants, and dress pants made in nearby garment factories, were for the most part first quality, though sometimes irregulars—meaning they had misprinted tags. And since it bought such huge quantities, Eckstein's got goods for less than retail stores did.

Eckstein's never did go electronic—no computerized cash register, no credit card swipes, no security cameras. But there was no lack of electricity inside the store emanating from the screaming workers and feisty customers endlessly arguing over prices. Mounds of jeans piled in the basement doubled as dressing-room curtains. Oftentimes, people who tried things on behind stacks of Wranglers, Lees, and Levi's also quietly stuffed their bags with unpurchased goods. And tax, when it was charged at all, was tabulated on a printed sheet taped to the counter.

Shoppers were discouraged from leaving the store without purchasing something. If Eckstein's didn't have the goose-down winter jacket a customer was looking for, a salesperson would try to convince her that she needed a pair of Dr. Denton's pajamas instead. If she walked out empty-handed, my great-uncle Herbert—who learned from his uncle Teddy—cried out to the salesman: "What happened? What do you mean she didn't want to buy anything? Lady, come back!" Then he'd beckon to another employee and write "second effort" on the back of a business card, compelling him to chase her into the street, follow her into another store, and offer her a better deal. In the end, the customer felt triumphant for having knocked the price down, and the store made another sale. And Herbert, who regularly refused to let customers out without inquiring about their marital status, often had a match for the single Jews.

Religion remained an important part of the lives of Orchard Street shopkeepers and workers, most of whom were Orthodox Jews. Since the employees seldom had time to take breaks and go to synagogue during the day, they could easily round up enough salesmen from nearby shops and hold a quick, ten-minute afternoon minyan (a prayer circle requiring ten men) in the back of a store. And on Sundays, the busiest day, neighborhood synagogues held seemingly round-the-clock yortzeits (services remembering departed relatives) for harried shoppers.

The stores closed down early Friday evening and stayed shut until sundown on Saturday to observe the Jewish Sabbath. But they gained an edge by illegally opening on Sundays in the days when "blue laws" kept stores closed. The blue laws were a holdover from seventeenth-century New Haven where Puritans wrote restrictions on blue paper preventing regular work, shopping, travel, sports, or public entertainment to give people a day of rest to observe the Christian Sabbath. Such restrictions were subsequently enforced to various degrees in the Tri-State area until the late 1970s. But with the Lower East Side shops observing their day of rest on Saturday, they collectively decided to flout the law and open on Sunday. The police would fine the stores every month, and every month owners would get together and choose a delegate to send to the courts to pay this nominal fee.

Commerce along Orchard Street was largely wholesale. "Jobbers," the freelancers of the mid-twentieth century, bought goods on the Lower East Side and sold them elsewhere, mostly to small stores in the city owned by other Jews or Italians. "Customer peddlers" bought goods weekly to resell to customers from their neighborhoods or workplaces. And street peddlers bought goods to sell from pushcarts or out of packs they walked around with on their backs.

Among the wholesale jobbers and peddlers who crowded the Lower East Side shops and kosher dairy eateries were men like Al Lattman, who grew up near Orchard Street. He became a customer peddler in 1928 at the age of eighteen to get some extra cash for playing the numbers games or betting on horses. Lattman later worked full-time at the post office but continued his side business selling clothes to his co-workers. Before heading to work in the morning, he would eat at Ratner's, the kosher dairy restaurant, and then wait in front of Eckstein's as the gates went up. Once inside, Lattman would pick out the clothes his co-workers or neighbors ordered. Then he'd hang around and regale the salesmen with stories of the neighborhood's illustrious former residents before heading to the post office. Lattman liked to schmooze with theater folks. He befriended Lower East Siders such as Julius Epstein, who wrote the screenplay for *Casablanca*, and gangster Bugsy Siegel. Workers and customers loved listening to Lattman, and Meyer even offered him a job in the store, but he refused. Still, Lattman was one of the few holdouts over the decades who continued to visit the store until he moved to Florida in the 1990s.

Another Orchard Street character who worked at Eckstein's for decades was Marcus, a large, loud man who oversaw towels and linens and was also charged with watching for shoplifters. Whenever he spotted one—and there was at least one a day—he would alert other workers with a howl. Eventually, the word "Marcus" became the code at Eckstein's for a potential thief.

"Red" Horowitz was a "finagler" who got into trouble with some Mafia guys after walking out of a brothel without paying. This indiscretion meant that two strong-arm men would show up at Eckstein's every Friday to collect on his debt.

And then there was Melvin, a short, portly Orthodox Jew who said his night job was being "Johnny Love" at a XXX club in Times Square. He also claimed to have all sorts of skills from his training as a Green Beret during the Vietnam War. One of these was performing a tracheotomy with a pen, which he said he did one night on the subway after he chopped at the jugular of a would-be mugger, then changed his mind and decided to save him with a pen.

Within a few years of opening the first shop, business was brisk and Eckstein's moved into a larger store on Orchard Street at the corner of Grand. Shortly after my grandfather David was born on Delancey Street in 1920, Meyer moved his family out of the Lower East Side tenements and into the brownstones of Brooklyn's

Bedford-Stuyvesant and then to a house in Crown Heights. But even when living in Brooklyn, Meyer would often work until midnight. During the Depression, he would walk across the Williamsburg Bridge after sundown on Saturday—a ritual followed by many Jewish Brooklynites—and open up the store to do some business. He'd also make some extra money in those years by selling everything he possibly could, including the crates the goods came in.

The 1930s were peak years for Lower East Side businesses, and during the Depression, Eckstein's had almost ninety workers, many of whom held onto those jobs for decades. But business took a blow when Mayor La Guardia's 1938 "slum clearance" efforts forced pushcart peddlers from the overcrowded sidewalks and into the stalls inside the Essex Street Market. Many established merchants, even though they, too, were immigrants, wanted to oust the peddlers from the streets. They viewed them as a public and personal embarrassment that reminded them of the Old Country ways they wanted to wash away. But without the pushcarts, the area lost some the nostalgic feel that drew former Lower East Siders and tourists to the area. The store owners soon missed the foot traffic the peddlers had helped generate. And with the peddlers gone, the merchants experienced a dramatic loss of sales.

Lower East Side businesses suffered further blows after World War II. Manufacturers began selling directly to retailers, eliminating the need for many of the wholesale jobbers who had shopped at stores like Eckstein's, which reduced the already thin profit margins for the merchants on Orchard Street. The dismantling of the elevated train along Allen Street and the razing of tenements to widen streets to make way for looming brick high-rise housing projects and the cooperative apartments for members of the Amalgamate Garment Worker's Union did little to boost street life. (And plans by "master builder" Robert Moses for the Lower Manhattan Expressway, which threatened to wipe out many tiny blocks of tenements, were fiercely fought by the merchants, and the expressway was never built.)

Nevertheless, Sunday sales continued to give stores like Eckstein's an advantage, attracting Jews and other shoppers from all parts of the metropolitan region. Jewish families came from the Grand Concourse in the Bronx, Flushing in Queens, and Manhattan Beach in Brooklyn. They came from Long Island and New Jersey. They shopped to stock their own dry-goods stores or for underwear and T-shirts by the dozen for their families. They would make a day of it, buying clothes, buying kosher candy, and eating at the kosher dairy restaurants, such as Ratner's and Rappaport's. The Lower East Side still felt like the epicenter of Jewish culture for many of the families who had moved out of the area, as well as for those who had never lived there. And the haggling in the stores was still an Old World comfort for many of these customers.

But after New York officially repealed its blue laws in June 1976, stores statewide gradually began opening on Sundays, eliminating the need to shop on the Lower East Side. That August, E. J. Korvettes, a major discount department store that had twenty New York City–area locations, was the first of the major chains in the city to open on Sunday. Soon to follow were Gimbels, Alexander's, and Macy's, where shoppers could buy goods in a haggle-free, hassle-free environment, pushing stores like Eckstein's further into the background for many shoppers. And once stores in New Jersey—where the state left the decision to repeal the blue laws up to its twenty-one counties—started opening for Sunday sales, the stores on Orchard Street took another hard hit. The lines that used to wind out of Lower East Side stores on Sunday became a thing of the past. But business remained steady up into the early 1980s because shoppers were still drawn to the Old World ambience and discount prices.

By the early 1980s, it was otherworldly to drive to the Lower East Side from our suburban home in Rockland County, away from the malls with Macy's where designer clothes hung neatly on racks, to watch people haggle over already cheap goods. By then the Lower East Side was becoming a haven for prostitutes and heroin users. Suburban shoppers looking to buy underwear and socks for their families didn't necessarily want to park in front of strung-out drug addicts hanging out in tenement doorways. To cut costs, Eckstein's began purchasing goods of questionable quality. One time Herbert went on a shopping spree of closeouts and stocked up on cheap sweatshirts in the most awful colors and chintzy ladies' sweaters, which the store ended up practically having to give away over the years.

The wholesale side of the business continued its downward spiral, although some peddlers, small shopkeepers, and people who needed dozens of items fast still shopped at Eckstein's. Many wholesale customers came from Trinidad and Tobago and Jamaica to buy for small stores they had on the islands. Others, who came because credit problems or bankruptcy issues kept them from getting accounts with manufacturers, often turned out to be disreputable. They would buy crate loads of jeans or jogging suits and write personal checks for thousands of dollars. And time and again, these checks would bounce and the inventory was unrecoverable.

More sales were lost in the 1990s as bargain hunters found underwear, pajamas, and sheets at the seemingly ubiquitous massive discount chain stores, such as Kmart and Target. Wal-Mart, which is still looking to move into the boroughs, calculates that New Yorkers are already spending $98 million a year at their big-box stores in New Jersey, Long Island, and Connecticut. A generation or two ago, suburbanites were flooding out of the city after 5 p.m. Today so many have moved back that the national discount chains are ready to serve them in the city. And once customers could buy jeans from neat displays in various fits and styles quickly and easily using their credit cards at an array of Gaps, buying jeans at a place like Eckstein's became obsolete.

In recent decades, many owners have closed their stores and moved to Florida, while their kids have gone to professional schools and taken white-collar jobs. A few of the old family-owned businesses hung on into the twenty-first century before ultimately closing. Chock, a hosiery store that opened in 1921, closed down after its owner, who inherited the store from his wife's father, passed away. Gorelick, another dry-goods store, recently closed when proprietor Bernie Gorelick decided it was time for him, his wife, and their sole employee—all in their eighties—to retire. Lizmore Hosiery, whose window display of Danskin tights remained virtually unchanged for nearly twenty years and whose owner would sit in a beach chair on the sidewalk whenever it was sunny and business was slow (sometimes holding a metal reflecting board underneath his face), eventually sold its building. The few remaining stores took another hit after the terrorist attacks of 9/11 when they lost a lot of clients from overseas—especially Africa and the Caribbean—who had still been coming for wholesale orders.

Gradually, nostalgia became the area's main currency and started to eclipse the actual stores. In 1988, the Tenement Museum moved onto Orchard Street and did a historic renovation of a tenement that still had bathtubs in the kitchen. The tourists coming to the museum, however, never seemed to venture much around the neighborhood apart from the official walking tour. So they never got to see the last days of the old-time stores or to peek into buildings—occupied mostly by Puerto Ricans and Chinese—that still had bathtubs in the kitchens.

While the museum's presence did little to reverse the tide of the old stores' ebbing sales, it did—along with rising rents citywide—help increase property values. Landlords of nearby buildings began renovating, either turning warehouses into luxury lofts or upgrading tenement apartments as soon as a long-term rent-stabilized tenant moved out. In a reversal of the area's earlier history, the apartments started to become hot commodities while retail spaces languished.

By the end, the only workers left at Eckstein's were family—my grandfather, my mother, and my brother. Recently some national chains have taken notice of this area's increasing real estate values and are moving in before the prices get too exorbitant. McDonald's and Burger King have been on Delancey Street for over a decade, but more recently Ratner's, which had been around since 1905, was replaced by a Sleepy's mattress store. Next came Starbucks. And a seventeen-story bright blue glass building designed by Bernard Tschumi is going up in Ratner's former parking lot.

When I spent days at Eckstein's during the 1980s, hookers and junkies made their home a few blocks away on Allen Street, Essex Street, and in Seward Park, which was the city's first established playground, built in 1903 to alleviate overcrowded conditions and lack of open space. Today, Seward Park has a colorful new children's playground frequented by nannies and their charges, where parents serve cranberry juice and other healthy treats at birthday parties.

The Lower East Side's streets are undeniably safer than they were even a decade ago. There's a growing bar, restaurant, and cafe scene on Orchard Street. A coffee shop that serves $7 prosciutto panini opened up, attracting young hipsters who spend hours reading or working on their laptops. A small restaurant is now serving gourmet pork chops and seared scallops with a drizzle of hazelnut sauce to an evening crowd of smartly dressed professionals. These restaurants would have been a *shande* (a source of shame) to the Yiddish-speaking kosher eaters of the old Lower East Side.

Some of the new places south of Delancey Street play on the area's history: the Lolita bar is named after one of the bra stores, and Barrio Chino, which specializes in tequila, takes its name from the Latino and Chinese residents who are being joined and sometimes squeezed out by the kinds of people who can afford to pay for $12 drinks at bars like that one. A hot dog restaurant and a vegan bakery (where cupcakes are made from spelt and cost $3.25) have recently opened, and a French bistro is renovating a space nearby. A pizza restaurant is moving in where Chock used to sell bras and underwear. These will attract some new, young residents with disposable incomes as well as those who are flocking to the little streets for the nightlife.

Now, some of the descendants of those who got started in the area and escaped it are moving back because the neighborhood still has human-scale buildings, small shops, and ethnic and socioeconomic diversity. But the real estate market is quickly pinning its hopes on this neighborhood becoming the next SoHo. Rent-stabilized apartments, where people are still paying a few hundred dollars a month, now share floors with renovated digs commanding rents of more than $1,500. The area's scale is slowly shifting as many developers buy up air rights of lower-rise adjacent buildings so they can build higher and higher. It seems as if luxury condos and rentals are going up on every available lot.

Those moving back to the city from the suburbs bring with them their suburban values and expectations of convenient and easy shopping (not to mention amenities such as concierges, gyms, and twenty-four-hour maintenance). With the Jewish immigrants hawking wares from pushcarts long gone and the family-owned stores dwindling, the foot traffic on Orchard Street is relatively ghostlike during the middle of the day. The high-priced one-of-a-kind outfits at Forward, a collective run by young fashion designers, don't attract a lot of pedestrians to its "please ring bell" storefront; nor does the recording studio on the street owned by a Japanese hip-hop DJ called Honda.

The newly organized Business Improvement District (BID) is trying to maintain clean streets by sending out a maintenance crew to pick up trash and repaint graffitied store gates. The building where I live still has toilets in the hallways for some apartments and still has groups of immigrant boarders squeezing together and subdividing tiny sleep spaces—there's one such apartment for a group of Fujianese men and one rented out by Arab men. Most of the other tenants are Cantonese, West Indian, and Puerto Rican families and a woman who used to be a part of the East Village party scene during the 1980s. When a Trinidadian man who had been living in the building for years passed away, the space was gutted and renovated with marble tile for the bathroom and in moved two young white men who listen to loud indie-rock music.

The BID has made noises about bringing back an open-air market to Orchard Street to lure visitors and further capitalize on the nostalgia that's been captured by the Tenement Museum, which has expanded in recent years. It's similar to what happened to Orchard Street's cobblestones: Some time in the late 1980s, the city paved over them. Then in the 1990s, the Tenement Museum got part of the block nationally recognized as a historic site and "re-cobblestoned" a fragment of it, but this time with smooth, neat red bricks that were never originally used in the area. These bricks make a gesture to the past, but they are nothing like the uneven, ankle-breaking cobblestones that were on the street originally. This new Lower East Side will most likely continue to reference the area's past, albeit from a safe, glossy distance and with a huge mark-up.

The BID continues to label the area as "the bargain district," but today's newly opened boutiques offer no bargains and have no patience for the lost art of haggling. Nor do these stores hire workers who will make their careers as salespeople and dedicate themselves to customer service as the workers at stores such as Eckstein's once did. After Eckstein's closed in 1998, the space was taken by Sheila's Decorating, a store that sells fabrics and reupholsters furniture. But the owner, an Orthodox Jewish woman, does most of her business online, not exactly something Uncle Teddy would understand.

DISAPPEARING ACTS
Harlem in Transition

Robin D. G. Kelley

Beneath the surface of the current Harlem-mania are the old signs and crumbling edifices that have yet to succumb to global capital's demolition ball. These signs, and the buildings to which they are attached, are not merely lost artifacts but declarations of war, holdouts that remind the observant passerby what black Harlem was and could have been. The ideas, visions, and hopes of the people in brownstone, brick, and mortar, in the official and unofficial graffiti that dot the urban landscape, reveal the signs of tension between capital's designs for this section of upper Manhattan and the designs of the residents.

History is contested, and for black residents, the glory that was Harlem was more than just a colorful backdrop to enhance neighborhood charm. On the contrary, the past has always been about charting a new future. After all, this place has been labeled "the Negro Mecca," once the most important black city in the entire world. It offered hope for a new beginning in an age of scientific racism barely two generations removed from slavery. It promised the flowering of a black intelligentsia and culture, a symbol of what sophisticated, urbane black people could become if they held power and were left alone. Indeed, it is precisely this sense of hope, possibility, dreams unrealized that explains why every generation since the early twentieth century laments the loss of "the old Harlem." James Baldwin's memories of the Harlem riots, Claude Brown's lamentations over the introduction of heroin and the rise of crime, Ralph Ellison's reminiscences of the old Minton's Playhouse, John Henrik Clarke's 1964 anthology *Harlem in Transition* all recall the golden age as a thing of the past.[1] But what was really lost and what will the new Harlem bring? To answer these questions, we need to dig even deeper beneath the surface and figure out how Harlem evolved from mecca to market.

"Are the Negroes Going to Be Able to Hold Harlem?" The great poet-critic James Weldon Johnson asked this question way back in 1925. Johnson knew that

Long-term Harlem residents have taken to the streets to protest the evictions of local families as Manhattan real estate values have risen to unimaginable levels and previously ungentrified areas have become prime targets for development.

the great black Renaissance would not last forever. He was less than sanguine about the black community's future in Harlem, predicting that an inevitable rise in land values would force black residents farther north and perhaps out of Manhattan altogether. At the same time, he believed that the success of Harlem's black middle class was irreversible, and if white folks had any plans to retake the old North Manhattan suburb, it would cost them. Johnson surmised:

> The Negro's situation in Harlem is without precedent in all his history in New York; never before has he been so securely anchored, never before has he owned the land, never before has he had so well-established community life. It is probable that land throughout the heart of Harlem will some day so increase in value that Negroes may not be able to hold it—although it is quite as probable that there will be some Negroes able to take full advantage of the increased values—and will be forced to make a move. But the next move, when it comes, will be unlike the others. It will not be a move made solely at the behest of someone else; it will be more in the nature of a bargain.[2]

Today Harlem is being overrun with bargain hunters in search of dilapidated brownstones and row houses, the kind of housing stock that allows one to make a dream home in an overcrowded real estate market or turn a quick profit through resale. The *New York Times*, *New York* magazine, the *Village Voice*, and virtually any publication with its eye on New York have pronounced Harlem the hottest real estate market in the city, thus adding to the skyrocketing value of property. Meanwhile, longtime black and Latino residents, from young mothers to the elderly to local entrepreneurs, are finding themselves on the losing end of the "bargain." Priced out and displaced, the old Harlemites who have for so long lurked in the white imagination as a source of fear and fascination have begun to disappear. And yet, this new army of developers, speculators, and investors marches through Harlem behind the wrecking ball of global capital, banking on the neighborhood's rich history as the center of black culture and art.

Anyone familiar with the transformation of Harlem today would find Johnson's prediction prescient, to say the least. In 1925, Harlem had been deemed by some the capital of the black world, where black artists, intellectuals, and entrepreneurs thrived, black police officers walked the beat, and black dreams need not be deferred. Of course, just three decades before the Harlem Renaissance, no one would have predicted that the choice block of land from 110th to 145th Street would become a predominantly black community, let alone the epicenter of the African Diaspora. By the turn of the twentieth century, Harlem had become the jewel in Manhattan's crown. Rising land values, boosted by the extension of the Interborough Rapid Transit (IRT) subwayline, attracted Manhattan's bourgeoisie along with a bevy of real estate speculators who erected beautiful brownstones, luxury apartment buildings, and a few small mansions. Oscar Hammerstein I, who made quite a fortune buying and selling Harlem property, built the Harlem Opera House with the assumption that the elite was there to stay. William Waldorf Astor must have believed the same, for he sank a cool $500,000 into a luxury apartment building on Seventh Avenue.[3]

When the editor of the *Harlem Monthly Review* observed that Harlem would become "the centre of fashion, wealth, culture, and intelligence," he was not thinking about Langston Hughes, W. E. B. Du Bois, Madame C. J. Walker, or other black Renaissance figures. Indeed, had you walked into most Harlem realty companies circa 1900, you would likely have found a sign on the wall that read: "The agents promise their tenants that these houses will be rented only to WHITE people." Or you might have seen the following attached to vacancy notices: "Keine Juden, und Keine Hunde" (No Jews, No Dogs). Yet, when the bottom fell out of the market, these same realtors sold to anyone willing to buy... and the rest, as they say, is history.[4]

At the dawn of the twenty-first century, this historic black working-class community threatens to become Manhattan's newest yuppie mecca. Developers and real estate agents who stand to gain a pretty penny are calling it the "second Harlem renaissance." Between 1990 and 1997, people moving into Harlem making over $75,000 increased by 80 percent, while families earning less than $10,000 decreased by 26 percent. But poverty still rules in Harlem. In 1999, the median family income was a paltry $18,000, and lots of folks were still living in overcrowded housing projects and struggling to find work. The unemployment rate hovered around 18 percent—four times the national average. In 2002, despite the influx of more middle- and high-income earners, the median family income rose slightly to $26,000 per year. Brownstones sell for $800,000 or more, and gutted brownstones begin at $300,000. Rents have tripled. Employed, stable residents who were renting apartments for $500 per month were suddenly being told that they would have to put out $1,300 to $1,500. In the new Harlem market, one would have to earn approximately $90,000 per year to afford what is considered moderate-income housing.[5]

Now there is nothing inherently wrong with rising property values. On the contrary, rising property values are generally good for community development, especially if a substantial portion of the community own their own property.[6] But for so long Harlem was a land of absentee landlords and tenants who lived near or below the poverty line. Without a strategy to create low-income housing units, the increase in property values and rents leads inevitably to massive displacement. During the 1980s, several Harlem churches took the initiative to build low-income housing units for working, poor families. Harlem Congregations for Community Development and the now defunct Harlem Development Corporation created 1,800 low-income housing units in city-owned buildings. Abyssinian Development Corporation (ADC), a project launched by Abyssinian Baptist Church under pastor Calvin O. Butts, also initially built low-income housing, although now ADC's primary investments are in building up the commercial strip on 125th Street and in attracting corporate interests. The city has become even less interested in the problem of housing the poor and low-wage working-class families. New York City's Housing Preservation Department (HPD) devotes much of its energy to encouraging and supporting high-income buyers. Ibo Balton, HPD director of Manhattan Planning, says that he envisions a process where young African Americans "who went to Yale can buy into Harlem."[7]

Harlem *has* attracted young black Yale graduates and other members of the rising black bourgeoisie. It is also attracting white settlers (the most famous being former President Clinton). Harlem's paler settlers are very much part of the story, for they have put a completely different spin on "white flight." Fleeing the more expensive parts of Manhattan, whites are integrating Harlem in large numbers. Unlike the integration of African Americans into white neighborhoods, where fear of declining property values compels white residents to fight (burning crosses, burning houses, mob violence) or flee altogether, whites moving into black communities tend to push property values up, thus pricing many longtime black residents out. It's funny how we never call this process integration; instead, we use the presumably race-neutral "gentrification." In Harlem, as with all other urban neighborhoods experiencing gentrification, white home buyers who move into predominantly black neighborhoods earn significantly more money than established residents, whereas black families who move into white neighborhoods tend to have the same incomes.[8]

The rise in Harlem's land value was fueled by a federal grant of $100 million and another $250 million in tax credits—the result of being designated an "empowerment zone" by the Clinton administration in 1994. The purpose of the Upper Manhattan Empowerment Zone (UMEZ) is to support capital investment and various business ventures in Harlem, although it has focused more energy on attracting outside corporate capital than building up local businesses. One of the UMEZ's big projects was the massive shopping center known as Harlem USA, which houses the Magic Johnson multiplex theater, an HMV record outlet, and the Disney Store. Harlem is now home to Starbucks, Old Navy, Gap, H&M, Marshalls, and several other global chains. The space now occupied by H&M and Marshalls was originally designated as the site for the Harlem International Trade Center, but Governor George Pataki and his supporters rejected the center, despite strong protests from local Harlem business people. In fact, Reverend Butts not only opposed the trade center, but he committed ADC to work with outside developers who built this multimillion dollar retail mall.[9]

To help prepare the way, Mayor Giuliani employed the police to make Harlem safe for big capital. On October 17, 1994, the same year Harlem became an empowerment zone, the mayor dispatched four hundred officers dressed in riot gear to remove the street vendors on 125th Street. These vendors, who had been selling their wares for three decades or more, represented a truly diasporic entrepreneurial class, with merchants hailing from West Africa and the Caribbean operating alongside native-born African Americans. Although conflict between "legitimate" businesses along 125th and the street vendors had been brewing since the 1970s, it is not an accident that the first military operations against them coincides with initiatives to woo Gap and Starbucks into opening shop in Harlem.[10]

Giuliani and the police also sought to prepare the ground for their new residents by stepping up the "war on drugs." Although much of Harlem was ravaged by the crack epidemic in the 1980s, the number of drug arrests has increased significantly in recent years despite a steady decline in drug use and violent crimes. Undercover officers are everywhere in Harlem, mostly engaged in "buy and bust" operations in which they randomly seek out dealers, make a purchase, and call their "field team" to execute the arrest. Their job is to essentially round up all the low-level dealers, including lookouts or addicts who earn vials of crack by simply finding customers. All of these initiatives are part of a general clearing of the land.

Whether intended or not, UMEZ orientation toward corporate developers and global chains, in combination with rising rents and a decline in pedestrian traffic due to the removal of vendors on 125th Street, has led to the destruction of local businesses. Copeland's restaurant has been an institution on 145th Street for over a quarter century. When owner Calvin T. Copeland tried to join new economic initiatives by opening a second eatery on 125th Street in 1996, the rising rents forced him to close down after less than two years. As soon as he vacated, Metropolitan Life Insurance opened an office in the space. Isis and Associates owned a store on 125th that sold books, greeting cards, and gifts. Ms. Isis's business was fairly lucrative, but within two years of Harlem becoming an empowerment zone, sales began dropping precipitously. By 1998, business declined by some 90 percent. Ms. Isis was very philosophical about the matter: "We've held the fort, we created the market, and now other people are going to come in and reap the benefits."[11] Leon Griffiths's Record Shack, a Harlem mainstay since the 1960s, was driven out by HMV. "They may bring jobs to the area," Griffiths mused, "but at the same time they are destroying our businesses....I live in Harlem. So the money that used to stay in the community is now leaving it, and we're losing control."[12] As Lloyd Williams, president of the Greater Harlem Chamber of Commerce, has pointed out, the majority of businesses on 125th Street are now owned by outsiders. "The number of people from this community who own anything on 125th Street you can count on one hand and still have a number of fingers left."[13]

The bigwigs overseeing the process of Harlem's economic "empowerment" have not shown much sympathy toward the small entrepreneurs. On the contrary, Deborah C. Wright, president and CEO of the UMEZ, and Barbara Askins, executive director of the 125th Street Business Improvement District, have taken a somewhat Darwinian free-market approach to the matter—only the strong survive, and that's the way it ought to be. As Askins explained, "If you can prepare yourself, if you can get that customer that Disney can draw to come into your store, then you can survive."[14] They also justify their policies by arguing that these big corporations are providing jobs and better quality services for Harlem residents. The problem, of course, is that the jobs in question are low-wage service positions that don't pay enough for employees to cover the rising rents in the neighborhood. And the loss of local business not only means the loss of capital that might have been reinvested in the community, but it can have an adverse effect on services. For example, when the corporate chain Duane Reade established a big store in Harlem, several local drugstores were driven out of business. The result has been fewer neighborhood drugstores, thus placing a greater burden on the elderly and infirm to travel for prescription drugs and related needs.

No matter how many chain stores and coffee bars find homes on 125th Street, Harlem's essential selling point remains the authentic black experience. The main attractions are all tied to Harlem's black history: the Studio Museum in Harlem, the Schomburg Center for Research in Black Culture, Sugar Hill, the home of Langston Hughes, the Abyssinian Baptist Church. Soon to be added to the list is Minton's Playhouse, the defunct jazz club in the old Hotel Cecil where bebop was allegedly born. The resurrection of Minton's is being made possible under the entrepreneurial hand of Robert De Niro (whose recent efforts to buy up Harlem deserve its own essay). Even in its most official form, Harlem pride is always black. The MTA's renovation of Harlem subway stations highlight colorful mosaics depicting historic figures such as Marcus Garvey and Thelonious Monk. Busloads of European and Japanese visitors flock to local churches on Sunday mornings and jazz clubs on Saturday nights, all in search of that authentic black experience. Ironically, the very conditions that facilitated tourism have contributed to the slow disappearance of the black working-class culture they seek. Recently, the owner of the Lenox Lounge on Malcolm X Boulevard complained about the lack of local patronage and observed that the tourists were "very disappointed because they are coming for our culture....They want to see how we pop our fingers and get with it, and they get in here, look around, and it's nothing but white folks."[15]

The site of the former White Cross Shoe Clinic is now a U.S. Army recruitment center. I cannot help but think of the irony of a place called White Cross signaling the death of Harlem when some eighty years ago, Marcus Garvey's Black Cross Nurses marched along these very streets with a mission of community uplift. The Black Cross Nurses, an auxiliary of the Universal Negro Improvement Association (UNIA), instilled black people with racial pride and ministered to the needs of black men, some dressed in military regalia in preparation for war with white supremacy. The UNIA (whose Harlem branch was the largest single branch in the world) preached entrepreneurship and black ownership of property and business in Harlem.[16]

If you go back to that spot today, you'll find a completely different projection of militarism in its place: the White Cross is now where the U.S. Army trolls for young men and women to send to war! Had I made up this story, I would be accused of being overbearing with symbolism and irony. Yet, this is the truth, a truth that isn't so absurd when we consider the fact that African Americans constitute nearly one-third of the U.S. Army. In an age of massive displacement, dislocation, and war, the army is poised to draw the young men and women who have few career opportunities in the new Harlem.

Neither military recruiters nor chain stores can smother Garvey's ghost. As long as he roams these streets, we should avoid making any grand pronouncements of Harlem's death, lest they be premature. Harlem, after all, is internationally renowned for fighting back. Harlem produced the New Negro "dying, but fighting back," Father Divine, the African Blood Brotherhood, the League of Darker Peoples, the Black Arts Movement. It was the place where intellectuals like Hubert Harrison, around the time of World War I, stood on a soapbox and rallied hundreds of black folk to causes for justice in Africa, India, Ireland, and the Philippines; where people read and discussed papers bearing names like *The Liberator, The Crusader, The Negro World, New Dispensation, Negro Champion,* and *The Messenger,* all holding on to a dream of freedom; where residents could walk to 135th Street and find one of the largest collections of materials on black history in the world, the Schomburg center.[17]

Harlem residents' sense of history, in other words, does not necessarily serve the interests of property. Today, tourists from around the world line up outside Sylvia's famous soul food restaurant and tiptoe around congregations in worship for a glimpse of the real deal, where veteran activists such as Sam Anderson and the late Bill Epton struggled to raise money to create a museum dedicated to Malcolm X. We shouldn't be surprised, for Malcolm's was the voice for keeping Harlem in black hands and creating a leadership body primarily interested in serving ordinary working-class residents. During the early 1960s, he organized a series of Unity rallies, criticized local politicians for not responding to the poor, and during the Harlem riot in 1964, argued that the real criminals were not the "looters" but the police and the merchants. His remark was unforgettable: "The press is used to make the victim look like the criminal and make the criminal look like the victim."[18] The Harlem chapter of the Progressive Labor Party went a step further, portraying the uprising as part of a broader anti-imperialist war. "Not only are the Black people in a rebellious state," announced a pamphlet titled *Black Liberation Now!*, "but we are more and more beginning to line up with the Vietnamese people and other oppressed peoples in the world who are fighting the common enemy—U.S. imperialism."[19]

This is not the sort of thing one finds in subway station mosaics or hears about from tour guides. Nevertheless, Harlem has long been seen as the American headquarters for black liberation. It is what brought Fidel Castro to the Hotel Theresa in 1960, what attracted visits from African leaders such as Sekou Touré of Guinea and Kwame Nkrumah of Ghana. It is what convinced a young poet named LeRoi Jones (soon to be Amiri Baraka) to relocate in 1964 and lead a contingent of black artists intent on making cultural revolution. And it was what persuaded young activists to hold the Million Youth March in Harlem on September 5, 1998. The leaders behind the transformation of Harlem did all they could to keep the march out. Manhattan Borough President Fields, perhaps the city's leading black woman elected official, believed it would be terrible for business: "The Harlem community has worked long and hard to bring about positive change in our neighborhood. We are now enjoying levels of tourism and economic investment that would have seemed impossible ten to fifteen years ago. Images of police officers in riot gear arresting young people of color broadcast over the nightly news would be tremendously damaging to the Harlem community and to the city as a whole." Although the damage to business was minimal, her prediction of police in riot gear certainly came to pass. After a high-tempered contest with the city over the right to hold the march in Harlem, the event took place under massive police presence. Just seconds after officially ending the march, riot police converged on the crowd, causing a melee.[20]

Daily life in Harlem, as I remember it at least, is an accumulation of miniature pains and frustrations alongside startling moments of beauty and laughter. Harlem has been a place our parents (frequently mothers) labored long hours simply to afford rotting produce from the corner grocers and to pay rent on substandard tenement apartments or dimly lit high-rise projects. Residents had to make a life in small places, crowded with siblings and pests, rusty tap water, radiators that worked intermittently during the coldest of winters, and few windows to relieve us from the summer heat. Of course, there were fire escapes—poor people's terraces—and innumerable ways to escape the fire of ghetto life. Harlem had its share of block parties—fire hydrants blasting cool water on overheated ashy-brown bodies—and corner candy stores where loose change bought you Pixie Stix, Good n' Plentys, caramel squares, jawbreakers, Red Ropes, and huge chunks of bubble gum. The authentic Harlem can be seen today in the dignity of elderly women walking to church and in uniformed school children whose smiles embody their parents' hopes and dreams of a better life for the next generation. I am sure that some aspects of the new Harlem will make these lives better, safer, even happier, while others will render them more difficult.

So, will the black working class hold on to Harlem? Did they ever have it to begin with? With all the congratulatory talk of Harlem's empowerment and rebirth, one would think we are witnessing the beginning of black Harlem's greatest moment. The late John Henrik Clarke, the extraordinary historian who remained devoted to Harlem from the time he arrived from Alabama during the Great Depression, believed the renewal of the community lay in the struggle against the selling of Harlem. A year before Harlem became an empowerment zone, Clarke described his home as "a community under siege, because of urban renewal, gentrification, and other designs to push the poor out of Manhattan Island." Yet, he reminds us of its long history of resistance and how that history has always been linked to the entire world. "The fight to save Harlem has already started. I am in this fight with a whole lot of people, some younger than I am, some older and a lot stronger than I am. I am of the belief that the generation that follows me deserves to see and live in a Harlem community that is intact."[21] This community still exhibits a beauty and power that refuses to disappear. Its daily life, dignity, and transformation can serve to inform new battles against the forces of commercialization, militarization, and Disneyfication.

Notes

1. James Baldwin, *Notes of a Native Son* (Boston: Beacon Press, 1984); Claude Brown, *Manchild in the Promised Land* (New York: Simon and Schuster, 1999); Ralph Ellison, "The Golden Age, Time Past," in *Shadow and Act* (New York: Signet, 1964), 198–210. The most recent exploration of the various myths surrounding Harlem's "golden age" is John L. Jackson, *Harlemworld: Doing Race and Class in Contemporary Black America* (Chicago: University of Chicago Press, 2001).

2. James Weldon Johnson, *Black Manhattan* (1930; repr., New York: Arno Press, 1968), 158–59.

3. Gilbert Osofsky, "The Making of a Ghetto" in *Harlem USA*, ed. John Henrik Clarke, 9–10 (New York: Collier Books, 1971), originally published in 1964 as *Harlem in Transition*. See also, Gilbert Osofsky, *Harlem: The Making of a Ghetto: Negro New York, 1890–1930* (New York: Harper and Row, 1963); Roi Ottley and William J. Weatherby, eds., *The Negro in New York: An Informal Social History, 1626–1940* (New York: Praeger, 1969); David Levering Lewis, *When Harlem Was in Vogue* (New York: Random House, 1981).

4. Osofsky, "The Making of a Ghetto," 9–11.

5. Guy Trebay, "The Harlem Shuffle," *Village Voice*, December 28, 1999, 27; Rivka Gewirtz Little, "The New Harlem," *Village Voice*, September 24, 2002, 51.

6. Mindy Thompson Fullilove, Lesley Green, and Robert E. Fullilove, "Building Momentum: An Ethnographic Study of Inner-City Redevelopment," *American Journal of Public Health* 89, no. 6 (June 1999), 840–44.

7. Mamadou Chinyelu, *Harlem Ain't Nothin' But a Third World Country: The Global Economy, Empowerment Zones and the Colonial Status of Africans in America* (New York: Mustard Seed Press, 1999), 47–48; Amy Waldman, "In Harlem's Ravaged Heart," *New York Times*, February 18, 2001; Younge, "Harlem—The New Theme Park," [Manchester] *Guardian*; Ibo quoted in Little, "The New Harlem."

8. Janny Scott, "White Flight, This Time toward Harlem; Newcomers and Good Times Bring Hope, and Fears of Displacement," *New York Times*, February 25, 2001; Monique Taylor, *Harlem Between Heaven and Hell* (Minneapolis: University of Minnesota Press, 2002).

9. Little, "The New Harlem," 51; Terry Pristin, "Harlem Development Program Not Much Help, Critics and Officials Say," *New York Times*, June 29, 2001; Chinyelu, *Harlem Ain't Nothin' But a Third World Country*, 47–48; J. Zangba Browne, "Harlem Reaps Rewards of Empowerment Zone Program," *New York Amsterdam News*, May 14, 1998.

10. Chinyelu, *Harlem Ain't Nothing But a Third World Country*, 75–78; Bryant Rollins, "Where I'm Coming From: Police vs. the 125th Street Merchants," *New York Amsterdam News*, March 3, 1972; Yusef Salaam, "125th Street Merchants Protests Giuliani's Slow Vendor Removal," *New York Amsterdam News*, October 1, 1994.

11. Kirk Johnson, "Uneasy Renaissance on Harlem's Street of Dreams," *New York Times*, March 1, 1998.

12. Younge, "Harlem—The New Theme Park."

13. Antonio Olivo, "As Clinton Moves in, Harlem Rents Go UP," *Chicago Sun-Times*, July 22, 2001.

14. Johnson, "Uneasy Renaissance."

15. Lynda Richardson, "Longing for Authenticity; Is the Jazz Really Jazz in Harlem without the Locals?" *New York Times*, November 16, 2000.

16. Ula Taylor, *The Veiled Garvey* (Chapel Hill: University of North Carolina Press, 2002); Barbara Bair, *Freedom Is Never a Final Act: Women Emerge from the Garvey Movement* (Chapel Hill: University of North Carolina Press, forthcoming); Robert Hill and Barbara Bair, eds., *Marcus Garvey: Life and Lessons* (Berkeley and Los Angeles: University of California Press, 1987); Winston James, *Holding Aloft the Banner of Ethiopia: Caribbean Radicalism in Early Twentieth-century America* (London and New York: Verso, 1998); Theodore Vincent, *Black Power and the Garvey Movement* (Berkeley, CA: Ramparts Press, 1971).

17. James, *Holding Aloft*; Theodore Kornweibel, *No Crystal Stair: Black Life and the Messenger, 1917–1928* (Westport, CT: Greenwood Press, 1975); Mark Naison, *Communists in Harlem During the Depression* (Urbana: University of Illinois Press, 1983).

18. Malcolm X, "Not Just An American Problem," in *Malcolm X: The Last Speeches*, ed. Bruce Perry, 161 (New York: Pathfinder Press, 1989).

19. Black Liberation Commission of the PLP, *Black Liberation Now!* (ca. 1966).

20. C. Virginia Fields, "In Million Youth March the Youth Come First," *New York Amsterdam News*, August 20–26, 1998; John Henrik Clarke, "Introduction," in *Harlem USA*, ed. John Henrik Clarke (New York: Collier Books, 1971), originally published in 1964 as *Harlem in Transition*.

21. Clarke, "Introduction."

SEVEN STOPS IN LOWER MANHATTAN
A Geographic Memoir

Lucy R. Lippard

New York City...always feels like the present.
—Kurt Andersen

The last time I visited my hometown—Lower Manhattan—a young woman emerged from the subway and asked me how to get to Bloomingdale's. We were on Spring Street and Sixth Avenue and I just laughed. Was *she* ever out of it. There could hardly be a *Bloomingdale's* anywhere near my home turf.

I was wrong, of course. Bloomingdale's and Old Navy have replaced the venerable Canal Jeans on lower Broadway. Hell, there's a K-Mart on Astor Place and there are two McDonald's within walking distance of my last urban home—which goes to show that I've been gone a long time, though I lived as an adult in Lower Manhattan for thirty-five years. When I was asked to think about the progress of suburbanization in the city, I spent a day in November 2004 walking my old neighborhoods, from one former home to another—a day that can be described only as nostalgic, a sentimental journey with a digital camera for company. So what follows is an entirely myopic memoir of seven urban sites in relation to their suburbanization...or not.

Although I was born at New York Hospital and lived on the far Upper East Side until I was nine, the geography during that part of my life was so different that I think of it in the same way as my other childhood homes in New Orleans, Charlottesville, and New Haven. By the time I returned to New York City in 1958, at age twenty-one, fresh out of college and stints in Europe and Mexico, there was no question in my mind about where to live: Greenwich Village was where artists and writers hung out.

Double-decker buses crammed with tourists glide along Spring Street in SoHo, a neighborhood of small-scale nineteenth-century manufacturing buildings that was colonized by artists in the 1970s and is now the home of high-priced boutiques, cafes, and restaurants.

75

I'd wandered self-consciously around Washington Square as a college kid, so, with two other recent graduates, I rented a tiny apartment on Washington Place, a pretty street just off Sixth Avenue, in the shadow of St. Joseph's church. I lasted only a few months there before falling for a homeless Beatnik-panhandler Zen Buddhist AWOL from the Navy as a peace protest, of whom my roommates heartily disapproved. By then I had discovered that Greenwich Village was just a commercial bohemia; the real artists had moved east of Astor Place, and the East Village was the place to be. The Tenth Street gallery scene was still vital when we moved to 436 East Ninth Street, just off Avenue A and Tompkins Square Park. I bought the lease for minimal key money from a junkie nephew of Archbishop Cushing, whom I'd met through friends at the Catholic Worker. The rent was $18 a month. It was a one-room "cold-water flat" with a closetlike bed space that was my study, a sink and a covered bathtub that doubled as a kitchen counter, and a shared toilet down the hall. When I unplugged the fireplace, I found newspapers from World War I and a Doughboy whiskey bottle. I bought an ancient decorated gas stove, which was immediately adopted by thousands of cockroaches that took up residence in the oven. They had the run of the place when I was out. When I returned, I learned to turn on the light and look away for a second while my roommates rushed back to their nests. When the oven was turned on, the exodus was reversed.

I painted a rug on the floor, borrowed an awful red canvas from a failing artist, and acquired a cat that walked in over my stomach one night from the fire escape. She had kittens in the fireplace and soon departed again. We formed a kind of commune with two other like-minded souls in the building, sharing Jim's icebox and my telephone. Nora, next door, the single mother of a little girl named Dylan, had very little in the way of worldly goods. She taught me to shoplift and contributed her talent for reading James Joyce out loud like an angel. I was the only one of us with a full-time job (at the Museum of Modern Art Library, for a hefty $45 a week), and I often fell asleep to chess games taking place on the floor next to my bed. Quart bottles of beer cooled on the sill. A sweet-smelling smoke permeated the air. In the blistering summer nights, we slept on the roof.

The halls smelled like drains. The streets were littered, and the facades were shabby. Latin music blared day and night. It was my first self-made home, and I was in heaven.

There was a drugstore on the corner of Avenue A. Poet Frank O'Hara lived across the street. Sometimes Allen Ginsberg, Jack Kerouac, Peter Orlovsky, et al. showed up at neighborhood parties. Some other political types from the Worker lived up the block. I bid farewell to Bermuda shorts and paisley dresses and assumed black tights and a ponytail. My first political protest was against the Lower

Manhattan Expressway, a prophetic attempt to bust up Lower Manhattan's communities. I helped a Puerto Rican guy across the hall install his icebox, and he returned the favor by protecting me from a stalker. Tompkins Square was still a haven for the many old Ukrainians in the neighborhood. (There was a Russian Baths a block away.) Sometimes, after an all-night party, I walked through the square around dawn. Stolid old couples, perhaps former farmers used to early rising, would already be ensconced side by side on the wooden benches, watching the day break.

This too lasted barely a year. Partly to escape from an ex-con I'd befriended, who was arrested for stalking me, I moved in with an abstract painter showing on Tenth Street and who lived on Avenue A and Eleventh Street, behind another building. We were robbed that summer, but the thief—apparently headed for the beach—took only a pair of Bob's sunglasses and a bottle of beer. Among our neighbors was a middle-aged couple, who had a cat named Zuni. Saul was building a sailboat in the basement with a special high cabin for his wife, who was badly crippled. (Later we actually survived a sail in this boat at City Island.)

Eleventh Street was too small for both of us and all my books. I had quit my job at MoMA and embarked on a lifetime of freelance research and writing. We found a cheap place at 278 East Seventh Street near Avenue D. It was a big, ugly gray tenement with a twin next door. The connecting basement was an underground railroad for major drug trade, and both buildings were rife with random burglaries. Whenever we came home and saw a small boy on one of the landings, we knew he was a lookout and wondered if we were the victims of the day. We were barricaded by all kinds of locks, but once they managed to break down the whole door. Finding nothing worth reselling, they scattered my extensive collection of worthless plastic "popit pearls" over all three rooms in disgust. (My typewriter, our lifeline, was stored in the covered bathtub beneath an array of dirty dishes guaranteed to scare off the undomesticated.) Still, it was a friendly neighborhood, with people speaking various languages, drinking beer, and playing dominos and cards on the sidewalks until all hours.

After about a year of this, we got married, and Bob found a studio at 163 Bowery near Delancey Street. Soon afterward we moved into it—a second-floor loft with huge windows in the front and a big dark studio space in the back. The landlord was asking $75 a month. Since that was beyond our means, we talked him into $65. On the floor above was a small business that made campaign buttons. (We commissioned one with Mona Lisa on it that we sold outside the Metropolitan Museum when the lady came to town.) The stamping machine was right over our table, and we got used to the daily whomp, whomp, whomp. More sound effects were provided by actual rat races between the stamped tin ceiling and the floor above.

Loft dwellers at the time were ingenious and illegal. Since there was no plumbing in the front of the loft, Bob built a sink on wheels, with a bucket beneath the drain, that could be rolled into the studio where the hot water was, and the bucket was emptied. The shower was on a very high platform because it drained through a hose into the toilet. While living on the Bowery, we had a son, Ethan. (If the baby had been a girl, she would have been named Delancey.) What had been the kitchen then became his room, and cooking was moved to the back. A restless mother, I strollered him all over downtown Manhattan. The city spirit came up from under the sidewalk at him, and he has never left.

There were a few artists on the Bowery then (1961–66), but it was not yet an industry. Between MoMA and the neighborhood, a tight community of young artists had formed (in prefeminist days I called us the Bowery Boys), which included several who have since become art-world household names. For the most part, however, the Bowery was still mostly flophouses, wholesale lighting and restaurant supply stores, and relatively harmless drunks, quaintly called Bowery bums. (Today, they would be the homeless; after the mental patients were kicked out of hospitals and dumped on the street in the 1970s, some were no longer harmless.) One morning I couldn't get out to work because a guy was slumped against the downstairs door at such an angle that it simply wouldn't open.

As a few paintings got sold and the marriage began to crumble, we could afford to have separate living quarters. Bob spent the summer of 1966 knocking down the walls between two tiny apartments at 46 Grand Street, between West Broadway and Thompson Street, and Ethan and I took possession in the fall. The now three-room apartment was on the top floor of a little building belonging to an artist. Grand Street was on the western edge of Little Italy, an exceptionally safe neighborhood because it was protected by the Mafia, who wanted no small-time crimes interfering with their broader activities. It was literally a parochial place. A babysitter lived across the street with no telephone, and we communicated by waves and yells. She belonged to St. Aloysius Catholic Parish—a church on West Broadway that was later torn down to make room for SoHo's first hotel. (I asked her if she knew some other Italian friends her age who lived a few blocks north. "Oh no," she replied, "*that's* St. Anthony's.")

A few days a week, we took a bus from West Broadway to East Broadway, to Ethan's preschool, the Educational Alliance, near the *Jewish Daily Forward*. There was a little public library across the street where I worked when I didn't have to help at the school, or I'd sit in Seward Park and watch that neighborhood unfold.

(In the 1980s, I often returned to East Broadway to conspire with a political artist friend who lived there. By then, the homeless had been pushed mercilessly east, along with the artists, as gentrification spread from the west.)

In 1968, friends asked if I wanted to come in on a new co-op loft building on the southeast corner of Prince Street and West Broadway. The maintenance fee was $125 a month. I was appalled, having never paid over $75. But the down payment was only around $5,000, and the space was great. I borrowed the money, thanks primarily to a friend who wouldn't get off my back about what a mistake it would be to turn this down. (He was *so* right; it's still the "family mansion.") The big red double building with eleven lofts was bought for a song, thanks to the fact that several of the artists involved were represented by Marilyn Fischbach's uptown gallery and her husband was a realtor. After the mortgage was paid off, we even *made* money off the ground-floor rents.

Three-year old Ethan and I (at thirty-one) moved into 138 Prince Street the same day the longtime furniture-finishing company moved out. As we went up in the elevator, the redheaded woman who was being evicted came down, justifiably pissed off at her displacement. Some of the other lofts in the building were still industrial, although SoHo (as it was beginning to be known, for "South of Houston Street," pronounced "Howston" to distinguish it from Texas) was less and less profitable for small industry. The guy who ran the freight elevator had a woman in the basement giving the workers lunch-break blowjobs. In 1968, lofts across the street were occupied by jazz master Ornette Coleman and an early lesbian organization, the Daughters of Bilitis.

My floor was black and encrusted with dirt and varnishes; the plumbing had to be taken out and replaced. For a year, we camped out in rotating rooms made of book boxes, pissed in a bucket, and cooked on a hot plate and toaster oven. Depressed by the filth and darkness, I began to wonder why on earth I needed a loft and was about to sell it to an artist friend when we painted the whole place white. Suddenly it was light and lovely. I decided to stay.

SoHo and NoHo were once called Hell's Hundred Acres, site of myriad sweatshops (still there in my day, hiring mostly Asian women). Just to the north, the infamous Triangle Shirtwaist Factory fire took place in 1911. When the historic preservationists discovered it, the area became known as the "cast-iron district," for the handsome old commercial buildings whose structural parts were mixed and matched from mail order catalogs. Our place was brick, and perhaps pre–Civil War, according to artist-architect Tony Smith.

In the late 1950s, when I first came to New York, there were artists already living in the neighborhood—not yet SoHo—but they were clandestine residents.

At night there were no streetlights, and windows were blacked out or curtained. When visitors came, you yelled up and the key was thrown out the window into the dark street, a loft-living ritual for many more years. Stoves, iceboxes, and beds were camouflaged or hidden, in case of fire department visits. By the time I moved to SoHo in 1968, the wraps were beginning to come off. Some small industries on the side streets hung in for years, but when rents skyrocketed, most of them were taken over by chichi furniture and clothing stores that occupied huge empty white spaces with a few black garments on a lonely rack. Now our graffiti-scrawled hallway is pristinely white. The dangerous, old freight elevator gave way years ago to a fancy little automatic. There's no longer the possibility of being hit on the head by a descending car or falling into the shaft when you look in to see what floor it was on.

The building next door on Prince Street was a big commercial bakery. Visitors often commented on how nice it must be to live next to that homey smell, but actually we were in danger of cinnamon silicosis, and the fat-lined chimney up the air shaft right outside Ethan's bedroom window would turn white hot and burst into flames. The smell came from barrels of Viennese Coffeecake Artificial Flavoring delivered weekly. Fumes from semis left running in the street were another part of the package. When I had meetings of the Artworkers' Coalition or the Ad Hoc Women Artists' Committee and its feminist rabble-rousing successors at my place, bakery workers offered free pies to attendees in miniskirts or tight jeans.

Little Italy, still primarily Italian, held its own in the smaller tenements and apartment buildings and small storefronts west of West Broadway, while artists held sway to the east, coexisting with older ethnic neighborhoods. On the two west corners of Prince and West Broadway were a bodega and a diner for the local workers. As the number of industrial workers decreased, middle-class artists increased. Although in SoHo's early art years we were a grubby and impecunious addition, we were new commerce, and the Italian neighborhood for the most part welcomed us. We thought this would be our place for a long time. As galleries appeared (Paula Cooper and Ivan Karp's OK Harris were first), we were glad to go to openings around the corner instead of getting dressed up and taking the subway to Fifty-seventh Street. The local bars were now our bars. Everything was in reach, from groceries to a bakery, a shoe store, cleaners, and a Laundromat, and there were four subways within walking distance.

In the 1970s, artists Gordon Matta Clark and Carol Gooden's restaurant Food opened a block up Prince Street. As SoHo became more prosperous, I got more of my furniture off the street, where it was abandoned by richer residents. A lot of people in suits and ties, even fur coats, began to show up. Later in the

1970s, the bakery closed and an art collector bought the building to use as a private museum, which never happened. Some Italian guys called Dean and DeLuca opened a small sandwich place, also on Prince Street. Fanelli's, the great old workers' bar on the corner of Prince and Mercer, became an art bar. There were "streetworks" (public art/political performances) on weekends and a lot of poster wheatpasting—capitalist and anticapitalist. You couldn't go out on the street without meeting people you knew.

But it wasn't "our neighborhood" for long. By the mid-1970s, the neighborhood was going downhill fast. My artist partner could hardly find a loft for $65, as we had in 1961—his studio was a windowless niche next to the boiler room in the basement of a nearby artist-owned loft building where he paid rent by working on the furnace. Most of us were blithely unaware of our role in this process, the fact that artists set off the gentrification of SoHo by paying higher rents, buying and refurbishing buildings, founding and showing at the new galleries that had moved downtown. After all, spaces were much larger, rents much cheaper. But even by 1970, the Saturday afternoon gallery parades looked ominous. Worse was in store. As more and more boutiques opened, the weekend "idiot parade" consisted more of shoppers than art lovers. I have to admit that we did not always resist the temptation to drop a raw egg or pitcher of water off our fire escape onto the invaders.

My entire sojourn on Prince Street was illegal. We lived in an industrially zoned building that was not up to code and did not have its certificate of occupancy. One morning around 1970, as I was getting breakfast and Ethan was still in his pajamas, there was a knock at the door. In my bathrobe, with eggs sizzling on the hot plate, I made the mistake of answering it. There stood two firemen who asked politely, "Do you live here, Ma'am?" "No," I said sweetly. They rolled their eyes and for some reason left us alone. I guess things had already gone too far. Later we got "artists in residence" status, but as I write we still don't have our C of O (certificate of occupancy).

The commercial ground floor of our building has reflected the changes. FCUK (French Connection UK), a hip clothing-store chain, now pays an astronomical rent that in turn pays the co-op's expenses. Virtually all of the small neighborhood businesses succumbed long ago to boutiques, souvenir shops, and schlock galleries. By the mid-1970s, the bodega and diner became a Swatch shop and an elegant jewelry store with an abstract mural on the facade. The ground floor of the bakery became a totally uptown jewelry store. Up the street, a ghastly many-breasted bronze sculpture towers over passersby. Luizzi's, the homey Italian restaurant where my kitchenless son and I ate so much we were practically family, has been the very expensive Raoul's for more than two decades. By the mid-1970s, we ate in Chinatown because we could no longer afford the "local" restaurants.

✳ ✳ ✳

When I returned to my former Lower Manhattan homes in 2004, I didn't know what to expect. My first apartment on Washington Place had changed very little in forty-six years, aside from a new paint job. Greenwich Village is still a haven for young middle-class college graduates, older families who have lived there all their adult lives, and a vibrant gay community. To my surprise, 436 East Ninth Street near Avenue A was still pretty run down, with a lot of graffiti on the buildings. The corner drugstore is now a club called Doc Holliday's with a Wild West mural on the Ninth Street facade. The block still harbors the kinds of funky shops that arrived in the late 1960s. Cat's Creative Claws Nail Salon seems to be flourishing, as are a funky dress shop, a Pilates and Gyrotonic, and a Turkish and Russian Baths (which survived the loss of the Ukrainian community). In the 1970s and even 1980s, the area was a "frontier"; artists moving in were considered "urban pioneers," as though no one had lived there before middle-class whites "discovered" it. And of course artists were welcomed by the absentee landlords where other poor people were not.

A cleaned-up Tompkins Square, on the other hand, is downright Victorian with its big shade trees and curving walkways—no sign of the tent cities of homeless protests in the 1980s and 1990s, the ubiquitous graffiti on the bandstand, the battles of artists and locals versus yuppies and developers that culminated in the Tompkins Square Riot, or the squatters' movement that survives but once ruled the area. In the 1960s, when I took Ethan to the playground there, I had to sift broken glass and hypodermic needles out of the sandbox. Now the play equipment is new and shiny, a list of rules is posted…but in the middle of the day, the playground was firmly locked.

Seventh Street and Avenue D is the surprise. The block is terminally spruced up, with new apartment buildings under construction, classier than Avenue A. The area is full of churches and a handsome old synagogue. The big gray twin buildings have been refurbished and don't look hospitable to drug deals anymore. Avenue C is honorifically labeled Loisaida Avenue (the longtime Puerto Rican nickname for the Lower East Side made official). The bar at Seventh Street and Avenue B where I once broke up with a lover is still there—I suspect the clientele has changed. A few blocks up, El Bohio Community Center, a huge old school and first home of PADD (Political Art Documentation/Distribution), my priority in the early 1980s, is boarded up. Nearby, Artmakers' La Lucha Continua, a community mural park, looks healthy, if overgrown, but it too is locked. Someone has crossed out Community Park and replaced it with Yuppie Catering Service.

There's a huge glass skyscraper on Astor Place, touted as "Sculpture for Living." There's a McDonald's on Delancey Street near our old Bowery loft, uneasily co-existing with the Templo Adventista Misionera and venerable Katz's Delicatessen. Despite the chain stores on Houston and Delancey, it is clear that the texture of Loisaida has been harder to rip than other parts of Lower Manhattan. There must be some persistent rent control, and the squatters' movement has managed to rescue and maintain some of the once-abandoned buildings. I found parts of Loisaida as vital as ever, but not necessarily the same parts. Allen Street, which I remembered as a rather gray, run-down avenue, is buzzing with restaurants and small shops. The vegetation in the median is flourishing, and even the once-ominous Eleanor Roosevelt Park looks like it's on its way up; a sign announces Closed at Dusk.

At 163 Bowery, our floor is now the home of the Malaysian Association of America. Like Golt Lighting below, its sign features Chinese characters. The retail stores look flashier, and many are Chinese, whereas previously they were old Lower East Side Jewish owned. I'm told by the younger generation that the Bowery is now known for clubs aimed at the Bridge-and-Tunnel crowd, the living spaces are increasingly posh, and once-low buildings are doubling in height.

Back west, the ground floor of 46 Grand Street—now absorbed by SoHo—sports the 46 Grand Bar and Lounge. On the corner of West Broadway is the upscale Felix restaurant. Three blocks up, 138 Prince Street is the center of a very different SoHo than the one I moved to in 1968. There are only a couple of "avant-garde" galleries left. They've all gone to bigger, whiter, chillier Chelsea and the trendy Meatpacking District. SoHo stores get more and more expensive. The chain stores on Prince itself (LaCoste, Coach, Phat Pharm) are not yet the big boxes, but on Broadway a few blocks east, Crate & Barrel, Pottery Barn, Staples, Armani, and Prada have replaced the homeless. The downtown Guggenheim Museum has decamped, and the New Museum of Contemporary Art is rebuilding at Prince and the Bowery. The vast gourmet food empire of Dean and DeLuca, a far cry from the little sandwich shop of yore, occupies a whole corner. Street vendors up and down Prince and Broadway sell scarves, hats, clothes, used books, jewelry, art, and tchotchkes to shoppers across the economic spectrum.

The old loft on Prince Street is now worth a ridiculous amount of money. Rupert Murdoch just sold his two floors across the street for an outrageous sum (in 2005, the block was cordoned off because Ariel Sharon was coming to visit). My god, how did this happen?

The neighborhood's downfall began when "loft living" became fashionable and doctors and lawyers arrived in the early 1970s. Some were refugees from suburbia and uptown rents, others were "trustafarians," others just wanted to be cool. It now seems inevitable that SoHo—a few blocks below Washington Square and NYU, near shopping meccas on Broadway, with such convenient transportation—would have become a desirable residential district. Artists were the flying wedge of gentrification that ruined SoHo for light industry. Then, with a certain poetic justice, SoHo was ruined for artists by the upscale newcomers we had attracted with our enviable, frugal lifestyles. (The same scenario has since played out in TriBeCa and Williamsburg; it remains to be seen where the creative capital will alight next.) By the late 1970s, SoHo was unaffordable for most artists who hadn't been able to buy in at an early date. Although we griped mightily and successfully organized for updated loft laws to accommodate live/work artist occupancy, most of us failed to understand the future of our "village" in the context of a rapidly globalizing economy and a changing city in which tax policy was manipulated to favor real estate developers.

As big money marched across Lower Manhattan, a few brave souls moved to the South Bronx, home in the late 1970s and early 1980s to innovative artists' spaces like Fashion Moda and then Longwood. At the same time, ABC No Rio and Group Material's East Side storefronts were outposts soon to become socially engaged islands in a changing scene. By the late 1980s, the Lower East Side was gentrified all the way over to Avenue D, chicly minimal gallery and boutique signs alternating with graffiti murals and political posters. A brief recession emptied some SoHo stores and some artists lost their lofts and galleries, but the economy bounced back, and in the 1990s, hard-pressed artists found studio alternatives in Long Island City (put on the map by the art-space P.S.1, which later became a far-flung outpost of MoMA), Staten Island, and Brooklyn, which now harbors several new "villages" and is colonized all the way to Bedford Stuyvesant, once a harsh ghetto. In the 1980s, when PADD organized a multisited street show called The Lower East Side Is Not for Sale, we were committed to the idea of a mixed-use, diversely populated urban community. In retrospect, I can see that our determined localism blinded us to the larger forces at work.

All over the country, there is a hopeful trend toward what a recent headline calls "New Life for Old Cities." Lower Manhattan, however, has never been close to death (or any closer to death than it was on September 11, 2001). Every decade, every generation rejuvenates the city by one means or another, fair and foul. New York is not Detroit. The dangers are not abandonment and decay but success and sellouts. Gentrification remains a more appropriate term for this area than suburbanization. So far as I know, my old turf remains free of the doorman-guarded condos that are the urban counterparts of gated communities. My own definition of suburban is a cocoon of homogeneity, isolation, and silence, but that preconception is a product of the 1950s. The suburbs have changed, getting browner and livelier as the city gets whiter and duller. It is no longer possible, if it ever was, to compare the suburban ideal of order and perfection with recalcitrant urban disorder and imperfection. As writer Rebecca Solnit has put it, the New Urbanists try to "design suburbs that resemble urban neighborhoods," while venerable cities are being designed to "function like suburbs." Lower Manhattan's "inner city"—a term that has become synonymous with drug-ridden poverty and dangerous, lousy schools, despite all the good citizens trying to make decent lives there—is always reinventing itself, and so are the suburbs. Yet as more and more poor people are shoved out, the colorful neighborhoods open to colonization by artists and their lucrative imitators are disappearing. Perhaps the suburbs are next.

Spend a day walking through Lower Manhattan. The energy is still there, and it's still seductive, even contagious. But only an acceleration of urban political activism will stem the tide of wealth and power that threatens to inundate my old neighborhoods.

THE TRIUMPH OF COMMERCE OVER COMMUNITY
A Look at New York City's Generic Street Fairs

Suzanne Wasserman

The ways in which the streets of the city are utilized by myriad New Yorkers has been contested for centuries. In the 1920s and 1930s, merchants and store owners led a campaign to remove open-air markets and pushcart peddlers from the streets of New York. In 1938, Mayor La Guardia successfully banned pushcart peddling and forever changed the uses of the streets. Well, maybe not forever...

Administration after adminstration has struggled with the ubiquity of street vendors and peddlers. The harshest response in recent years came from the Giuliani adminstration when the mayor specifically targeted them in his "quality of life" campaign. In the 1990s, he was determined to clear the streets of New York, first of the homeless, then street artists and musicians, and finally the vendors. Disputes over vending and peddling erupted in Midtown, Harlem, Chinatown, Washington Heights, Flatbush, and the Lower East Side. The battle reached a crescendo in the spring of 1998, and the media dubbed it "The Hot-Dog Wars."

That spring the Giuliani administration attempted to ban food carts from 144 blocks of Manhattan, including nearly the entire financial district and two large sections of Midtown. On June 4, 1998, close to one thousand vendors shut down their carts and took their protest to the streets. In an uncharacteristic move, Giuliani rescinded the order and backed off.

Far from being community events, street fairs today are an excuse for a collection of vendors to peddle their uninspiring food and wares, as was the case at the NYC Oktoberfest on Lexington Avenue between Forty-second and Fifty-seventh streets.

87

Interestingly though, within the last two decades one area of vending has been allowed to exist and even flourish—the ubiquitous and generic street fair. Over the past twenty years, the streets have become increasingly congested in the months between April and November when the fairs hit the sidewalks of New York.

New York is a city of neighborhoods. Manhattanites refer to where they live by their neighborhood's name—the Lower East Side, the Upper West Side, or Harlem, for example. Residents of Queens receive mail addressed to Douglaston or Jackson Heights, not to Queens, and Brooklynites know the precise borders between Cobble and Boerum Hills. Of course, over the years, New Yorkers' sense of community has been capitalized upon by an ever-burgeoning real estate market. It has created faux names for neighborhoods such as TriBeCa (Triangle below Canal Street), NoLIta (North of Little Italy), DUMBO (Down Under the Manhattan Bridge Overpass), and the latest, G-Slope, for the neighborhood surrounding the Gowanus Canal in Brooklyn.

Yet despite real estate ploys, a genuine sense of place pervades New York City neighborhoods. In some, this sense of community has been rooted in neighborhood associations, many of which originated in the troubled times of the 1970s. During the city's fiscal crisis, embattled neighborhoods began to establish block associations. Groups such as that on Bedford Street in the far West Village fought to take back the streets from drug dealers and users and to figure out ways to beautify their blocks in a city that could spare no extra funds. In those days, any block association could sponsor a street fair to raise some money for needed improvements. All that was required was a request to the city for a street closing. And anyone who wanted to put a table up could sell. Vendors simply signed up, sent the association a nominal fee, and showed up on the day of the fair.

Kathryn Donaldson, president of the Bedford-Barrow-Commerce Block Association, became active with the group as a way to meet people when she moved to the city thirty-two years ago. She immediately got involved in the planning of the association's annual street fair. It was a homey, all-volunteer street party organized by a hodgepodge of folks who put in a great deal of effort. They got wine from a local restaurant. Donaldson brought the hot dogs herself (and the local supermarket, Gristedes, would send over more if needed). They got tables and chairs from St. Luke's Church and dragged them all the way back at the end of the fair. A band made up of kids who called themselves The Sledge played dance music. And every year, for the past thirty-two years, the association has continued to sponsor its street fair on the third Saturday in May.

Fast forward three decades. It's a sunny day in mid-November and I am on my way to a meeting downtown. I decide to take the bus and give myself plenty of time. As we approach the Brooklyn Bridge, traffic grinds to a near halt. The bus driver announces that Water Street has been closed off and his bus will have to make a detour onto FDR Drive and will not stop until it reaches South Ferry. Everyone exits the bus. Alarmed, I wonder if there has been another terrorist attack, a water-main break, or a major drug bust. As I approach Water Street on foot, a sickly sweet smell wafts through the air. I hear the faint sounds of a Musak version of Simon and Garfunkel's "Bridge over Troubled Water." Then I realize it's a Veterans Day street fair!

I take note of the all-too familiar stands selling NY Candy Apple, socks, T-shirts and sweatshirts, sunglasses, $3 and $5 gloves, perfume, Souvla King Gyros, Anergy Smart Fruit Smoothies, Tres Bon French Crepes, Philly Cheese Steak, Maison Crepes, Kettle Korn, scented candles, jewelry, Italian sausage, $5 pash-minas, cell phone accessories for $5 and up, Hines Sweet Corn and mozzarella arepas, and Guatemalan ponchos.

A few days earlier I had stumbled upon a fair on Park Avenue South be-tween Seventeenth and Twenty-third streets, where I had seen many of the same vendors. I looked carefully for any booth that declared who was sponsoring the event. I asked one of the vendors, who replied, "Oh, this is produced by Mardi Gras Productions." After a bit of research, I learned that it was the Park Avenue South Autumn Fair, putatively sponsored by the Manhattan Republican Club. But the Manhattan Republican Club was nowhere to be found.

This experience can be repeated over and over and over again on New York City streets from early spring until late fall. Vendors sell the same food, the same cheap merchandise (most of it readily available at the suburban-style, big-box discount retailers popping up all over the city), and offer sign-ups for credit cards and newspapers. Every fair looks almost exactly the same. And there are a lot of them. In 2005, in fact, the city issued 388 permits for street fairs in the five bor-oughs—that is an average of more than one fair for every day of the week for an entire year! And neighbors have begun to complain that these "summer reruns" are crowding out the community.[1]

On a single weekend in June 2005, for example, one could go to the Sixth Precinct Community Council Fair on Bleecker Street between Seventh and Eighth avenues, the Stuyvesant Park Neighborhood–Second Avenue Fair on Second Avenue between Fourteenth and Twenty-third streets, the Lennox Hill Neighborhood House Fair on First Avenue between Sixty-eighth and Seventy-ninth streets, the 116th Street Festival (El Abrazo Fraternal) on 116th Street between Lexington and Third, the Big Apple BBQ Block Party–Madison Square Park on Madison Avenue between Twenty-third and Twenty-fifth streets, the Friends of Community Board

#2—Astor Place Festival on Astor Place between Broadway and Lafayette Street, the Christopher East Block Association Festival on Christopher Street between Seventh and Greenwich avenues, and the Tilden Midtown Democratic Club/New York City Expo on Third Avenue between Twenty-third and Thirty-fourth streets. That's just in Manhattan alone! And that's counting only the stationary street fairs, not parades!

By the end of the summer, the fairs are still going strong. On a weekend in September 2005, you could have visited the Great Irish Festival on Avenue of the Americas between Forty-second and Fifty-sixth streets, the Village Center for Care Fair on Bleecker Street between Seventh and Eighth avenues, Broadway on Broadway on Times Square at the intersection of Broadway and Seventh Avenue between Forty-third and Forty-eighth streets, the Tudor City Association Fair on Second Avenue between Forty-third and Fifty-third streets, the Columbus Avenue Fair on Columbus Avenue between Sixty-sixth and Eighty-sixth streets, the Ninty-second Street Y Festival on Lexington Avenue between Seventy-ninth and Ninety-sixth streets, and the Mexican Independence Day Festival on 116th Street between Lexington and Second Avenue. As Brian Lehrer writes in an op-ed piece in the *New York Times*, these fairs have come to represent "the triumph of commerce over culture, the marginalization of community in the name of community."[2]

It is the rare fair that still reflects any sense of place. One that does is the annual Ukrainian Festival started in the East Village in 1976 and sponsored by St. George Ukrainian Catholic Church. The fair features Ukrainian food (*varenyky*, *kovbasa*, stuffed cabbage, and home-baked goods) and offers Ukrainian arts and crafts (embroideries, wood carvings, ceramics, and traditional Ukrainian Easter eggs called *pysanky*). The Ukrainian chorus, Dumka of New York, gives a concert of sacred Ukrainian music, and dancers perform the traditional *hopak* and other folk-dance favorites.[3]

What has happened to the traditional neighborhood-association street fair? Why are these cookie-cutter fairs allowed to persist? And why are they encouraged when other street vendors are routinely routed and persecuted? The change came in the 1970s with Mayor Koch, who established the Community Assistance Unit (CAU). No longer willing to simply close streets for nonprofit organizations and pay for police and sanitation, the city saw fairs as a way to generate revenue. That was the death knell for locally controlled street fairs rooted in the neighborhood.

The CAU began to charge fair sponsors a 20 percent tax, a fee based on the price of the vendor space. For example, if the nonprofit sponsoring the fair charges $125 for a space, it takes $25 of that and sets it aside for CAU. Street fairs have become a cash cow for the city with the surplus flowing to the general fund. Instead of all proceeds going directly to the community groups, neighborhood associations found themselves paying the city for the privilege of raising money for their neighborhoods. Since 1995 alone, the city has raked in $10 million in vendor fees.[4]

At the same time the city began to make money from the street fairs, the process became overly bureaucratized. The red tape involved overwhelmed the volunteers who traditionally did their own planning. In the 1970s, when the city didn't have money to buy street trees or otherwise beautify neighborhoods, Donaldson and fellow members of the Bedford-Barron-Commerce Block Association used the proceeds of their street fair to buy their own trees. But now, rather than being encouraged and assisted by the city, they see themselves being discouraged and penalized by it. One year they got so demoralized, they actually cancelled their fair. But members soon realized they couldn't fight City Hall, so they gave in and filled out the forms, a very time-consuming endeavor.

Once the process of negotiating the bureaucracy and obtaining the necessary permits became formidable, middlemen immediately saw an opportunity and stepped in. There was money to be made, and the street-fair-and-festival promotion business was born. Only a nonprofit organization could request a street closing from the city, so the festival producers made deals with the nonprofits. They offered to negotiate the bureaucracy, but for a price. Nonprofits pay them to arrange for the permits, sanitation, security, and vendors, and the promoters take as much as 60 percent of the proceeds.[5]

The largest festival producers are Mort and Ray Productions, Clearwater, and Mardi Gras Productions. Mardi Gras's Web site proclaims,

> NYC Streets Are Paved with Gold. Street festivals generate mega dollars for vendors and corporate sponsors. Dollar for dollar, there is no more efficient way to promote your product or program than by bringing it directly to the public...[We] are now the no. 1 production company specializing in the placement of corporate displays...in New York City street festival venues.

They claim to be the "largest street festival producers in the USA." Mort and Ray Productions, established in 1976, claims to be New York City's "oldest and best known events company." It asserts that more than three million people attended their events in 2004.

The practices of the promoters have contributed to the generic flavor of the fairs. Not only do they fill out the necessary paperwork, they also have taken over the job of selling the vendors space in the fairs they organize. Vendors all sign up with the promoters in January or February for the entire year. And if vendors reserve a booth at more than one fair, they get a discount. Mardi Gras, for example, charges $150 to set up a single booth. But if a vendor commits to twenty fairs, the price drops to $115. The result is that the same T-shirt company turns up at fair after fair, which does nothing to promote local businesses or create a sense of community.

In order to hold a street fair, the nonprofit group is required to have a physical presence somewhere on the street. But many community groups ignore this requirement, leaving it virtually impossible to tell who is sponsoring a particular fair. On my visit to the Park Avenue South Autumn Fair, there was no sign of the Manhattan Republican Club. Neither could I find the Gramercy Stuyvesant Independent Democrats who sponsored the street fair on Broadway between Seventeenth and Twenty-third streets a week later. Because it has become harder and harder for community groups to work without a promoter, many nonprofits have abdicated the original mission of the fair, which was to make money *and* to promote a sense of community.

It also has become almost impossible for a new community group to apply for a permit. Today, the Street Activity Permit Office of the Mayor's Community Assistance Unit is responsible for regulating street fairs. But the number of fairs permitted has been capped with little likelihood of future openings, and city policy grants seniority to those who have been given permits before. "That means," writes Lehrer, "today's fairs will be tomorrow's fairs will be forever's fairs."[6]

The professional promoters also have become creative, figuring out how to cut the city out of profits by exploiting loopholes. Those block fairs that last only one day and take place on only one block can apply to their local community board instead of the CAU. If the fair is only a block long, they don't have to pay any city tax. Professional promoters have figured out that you can cram many more vendors onto a wide avenue than onto a tiny side street. This discriminates against neighborhoods like Greenwich Village where side streets are narrow. A fair that takes place on an avenue and stays within a block is a sure moneymaker for promoters. For one block, one day, the promoter pays no taxes.

The Bedford Street fair still tries to retain some of its individual flavor, and it is clear who the sponsor is. Block association members still run their own craft section, have their own outdoor cafe, and still have live music and dancing. There is no professional organizer involved, and everyone knows who's running it. Each year the Bedford Street fair makes about $25,000. Half goes to local groups and charities and half to buy trees and for tree maintenance, which includes tree guards and tree-guard repairs, pruning, plantings, a gardener to clean and water tree pits during the summer months, and deep root feeding. Over the years, they have given away more than $300,000. But fairs like the one on Bedford Street are increasingly a thing of the past and may altogether disappear. Donaldson is growing weary of the hassle and isn't sure how much longer she can convince her neighbors to continue to take on all the work required.

Every spring editorials and articles appear bemoaning the passing of the old street fairs and the proliferation of more and more generic ones. As Marcus Banks writes in the *Gotham Gazette*:

My wife and I reside in Yorkville, and one Saturday in June we attended a block party on East 87th Street to raise funds for the school at St. Joseph's parish. St. Joseph's has deep roots in Yorkville—it started before the Civil War as a place of worship for an orphanage and became the church for Yorkville's burgeoning German community in 1874—and this was evident in the June fair. A boy who attends St. Joseph's school staffed a table selling used books. Another table functioned as a one-day "St. Joseph's Café"—full of goodies baked by the school's parents or donated by local stores. There were children's rides and a dunk tank. There was not one single place to purchase a tacky souvenir glass. It felt much better to attend a block party that was clearly a part of its neighborhood, and buy a book to support a neighborhood institution, than it would have to eat a sickening sausage at a roving shopping mall.[7]

It's not the fairs per se that offend, but rather their contribution to the ever-expanding conformity of city streets. The booths that line the fairs are a cross between county fairs and suburban malls. As Lehrer writes, "The fairs were destinations. Today, you just run into them." There is something particularly anti-New York about them; what is missing is what journalists and writers used to call "local color."

If you look closely, though, you sometimes get a glimpse of the old New York flavor. At one fair, I noticed a unique Peruvian food stand. The vendors had set up an amazing grilling station made out of a metal cage where they roasted meat over a real wood fire.

Many of the vendors are recent immigrants who often supplement their incomes by working at fairs, and that fact in itself somewhat redeems the street fairs. An article in *Newsday* told of Marcos Sanchez, a recent immigrant from Mexico, who, with his brothers, cousins, and in-laws, works as many fairs as possible to earn money to send to family members back home in Mexico. While he was working selling sheets at the Kiwanis Club fair in Glendale, Queens, relatives staffed four booths at a fair in Brooklyn. But even he complained that the fairs were rather dull. "In Mexico, there are lots of games and music...It's much more fun in Mexico."[8]

Recently, anti–street fair activists, such as Edy Selman, a literary agent and member of the Washington Place Block Association in Greenwich Village, and Susan Goren, a member of Community Board #2's street fair committee, have emerged. For more than six years, they and others have fought the proliferation of street fairs. In 2003, they counted fifteen fairs in their neighborhood alone. The next year, another group of residents along University Place in the Village was so tired of yet another pointless fair disrupting normal street life that it circulated a petition against it. Even the president of Clearview Festival Productions was sympathetic. Todd Berman said his company strives to be considerate of neighbors. Alcohol and amplified music are prohibited, and vendors can't set up before 9 a.m. Problems arise when the events are clustered back to back. "I don't blame the [people] for being upset," he said. "That's wrong. They should be placed appropriately apart."[9]

The other main protagonists in the battle over street fairs are local store owners and businessmen. Merchants and street vendors have long squared off over use of the streets. Not surprisingly, store owners today feel that street fairs take customers away from local shops and hurt their business.[10]

Are there solutions to this problem, which, along with others, threatens the individuality of New York City's neighborhoods and thus the city's uniqueness in general? Lehrer suggests that sponsors should be forced to reserve spots for local merchants or subsidize young artists. "Today, [the fairs] are just another cog in the economy, posing as part of the neighborhood. They should be at least partly about the streets they are on." Last spring, the Fifth Avenue Merchants' Association in Brooklyn's Park Slope worked with Clearview to set aside an area for local artists and businesses. Maybe there is a movement afoot to reclaim the streets. As Lehrer suggests, "As street fairs once helped reclaim blocks, the blocks should now save the fairs from themselves."[11]

Notes

1. Sarah Garland, "Street Fairs' Big Bite: Neighbors Call Festivals Summer Reruns that Crowd out Community," *Newsday* (NY), June 12, 2005, G02.

2. Brian Lehrer, "Make the Street Fairs Less Generic," *New York Times*, January 4, 2004, Op-ed, 7.

3. Taras Schumylowych, "A Ukrainian Summer: Where to Go, What to Do...Begin the Season with New York's St. George Ukrainian Street Festival," *Ukrainian Weekly* LXXII, no. 18 (May 2, 2004).

4. Lehrer, "Make the Street Fairs Less Generic," 7.

5. Carrie Melago, "Merchants Gripe About Block Fairs on University Place," *New York Daily News*, September 9, 2003, 67.

6. Lehrer, "Make the Street Fairs Less Generic," 7.

7. Marcus Banks, "Block Parties, Street Fairs, Street Festivals," *Gotham Gazette*, August 2005.

8. Garland, "Street Fairs' Big Bite," G02.

9. Melago, "Merchants Gripe," 67.

10. Raphael Stern, "Heavy Street Fair Season Hurting Local Businesses," *Town and Village*, August 15, 2005.

11. Lehrer, "Make the Street Fairs Less Generic," 7.

IN THE CITY OF PERPETUAL ARRIVAL

Robert Neuwirth

Put it this way: Komal Ramparsad is my grandfather. This would come as strange news to Komal, who's more than ten years younger than I am, from a different part of the world, and Hindu, not Jewish. But it's true, one hundred years on, he's doing what my grandfather did, in almost exactly the same place. There's no denying it, he's more like my grandfather than I am.

My mother's father, Barnet Melnick, arrived in New York after a series of pogroms in 1905 made life impossible in Czarist Russia. He came to the city seeking opportunity. What he got was a miserable job as a sewing machine operator in a sweatshop. But he was a frugal guy and saved enough to open a candy store/soda fountain underneath the elevated train (the "El") in Cypress Hills, Brooklyn. It was a German neighborhood then, but my grandfather decided that in this diverse new land, nationality mattered less than location.

The myth in my family for many years after my grandfather sold the business was that the old neighborhood had become a slum. But it wasn't true. This modest neighborhood where the soundtrack of life is the shrill shriek of the El as trains traverse the sharp curve from Fulton to Crescent has remained what it was: a home to immigrant dreams. It only changed ethnicities, becoming less European and more Latino and West Indian. Today, Cypress Hills is where you will find Komal Ramparsad, manning the counter in a West Indian grocery one block from the soda fountain my grandfather ran for four decades.

Ramparsad came to New York six years ago from Guyana. He, too, came to create a better life for himself. "When you have a home there," he says, "you can work but you make no money." What's more, he said, Guyana has its own home-grown discrimination. "You have a kind of racialism between the blacks and the Indians." New York, for Ramparsad, is far less tense than his home country.

The extreme makeover of New York into a safe and prosperous suburbanized city tells only half of the story. Without the influx of new immigrants, New York would be shrinking, with many of its neighborhoods failing and its tax base eroding.

Today, at age thirty-four, he claims he has found a new identity and has no interest in returning to Guyana, even though his parents and siblings remain there. "I feel more American than Guyanan," he says as he banters with the few customers who stroll in on a brisk December morning. As they chat and pick through piles of freshly delivered eggplant, bok choy, young squash, and long beans—displayed in their cardboard packing cases—plus a wide variety of spices and curry powders and stacks of CDs and DVDs of the latest Bollywood beauties, the lilt of their English is so lush and musical that I find it hard to understand. After the customers move on, Komal continues his story. "Here you have a mix of everything. Every year, different people take over and different things happen. Fresh memory, fresh everything. I love everything here. I even love the winter." Komal has become a New Yorker. And, though it would no doubt embarrass him to say so, in this process, he has helped save his adopted city.

According to the common myth, New York has been revitalized through gentrification, which reclaimed the battered buildings and neighborhoods of a city that was given up for dead a generation ago. The casual consumer of news would be left to think that New York's economy is booming because of the good works and megadollars of developers and yuppie types, whose high-priced condos and suburban shop-till-you-drop lifestyle seem to be taking over the city. Immigrants, by contrast, are viewed as a drain on the city, sucking up services, subsidies, and Section 8 and destroying the civility and beauty of neighborhoods.

Contrary to these parallel legends, however, Ramparsad and his fellow recent arrivals are the ones keeping New York City alive. The upper-crust New York mainlined into the national psyche in sitcoms and serials like *Seinfeld* and *Sex in the City* is not the real New York. Outside of a few privileged neighborhoods, the average New Yorker is more like Ramparsad than Kramer or Carrie Bradshaw.

According to most economic indicators, the 1990s were a boom time for the city. Business thrived, rents soared, and Wall Street was in the stratosphere. Yet, while political leaders pretended everything was rosy, 1.3 million people left the city—and only 250,000 folks from elsewhere in the United States arrived to take their place.[1] This net outflow of more than a million people would have sapped the city, in both symbolic and serious ways. New York would have shrunk to around 6 million people—smaller than the city has been since 1920. Neighborhoods throughout the five boroughs would be feeling the effects of this contraction, just as they did in the 1970s, when New York's population plummeted by more than 800,000: abandonment, foreclosures, business failures, crime, a government response that led to the decay of infrastructure (through what policy makers called "deferred maintenance"), and, ultimately, to 1977's financial meltdown and default.

New York escaped this fate in the 1990s for one major reason: because Ramparsad and 1.2 million others like him arrived from abroad and decided to stay. Add to that 500,000 more births than deaths during the decade—because immigrants tend to have more kids than native-born residents—and you've explained New York's astounding recent population growth.

The strength of immigration in New York in the 1980s and 1990s far outpaced the fabled influx in the forty years from 1880 and 1920, when 1.5 million immigrants arrived from eastern and southern Europe. Between 1980 and 2000, more than 2 million immigrants poured into New York, one-third of them from the Caribbean and Latin America. In modern-day New York City, the 369,186 immigrants from the Dominican Republic make up the largest portion of the foreign-born population. Rounding out the "top-five" feeder countries for the city are China (261,551), Jamaica (178,922), the states of the former Soviet Union (163,829), and Guyana (130,647). Mexico and Ecuador are coming on strong, too.

Despite recent indications that immigration is tailing off,[2] city planners believe that immigrants will continue to flock to New York. "Despite 9/11 and despite the more stringent visa requirements we have, we assume that at the very least, the number of new immigrants coming to New York City will still be over 100,000 a year," says Arun Peter Lobo, deputy director of the New York City Department of City Planning's Population Division. The New York Metropolitan Transportation Council, a consortium of regional governments, projects that the city's population—currently 8.2 million—will vault past 9 million within fifteen years and will hit 9.5 million by 2030.

The dense array of skyscrapers may remain the postcard image of New York, but the city's real growth isn't in the borough residents call "the city." During the 1990s, Manhattan added only 50,000 additional residents—a population increase of just 3.3 percent. And most of those new arrivals were concentrated at the far northern tip of the borough, in Washington Heights and Inwood, neighborhoods that have long been a Dominican enclave.

The real story was off the island of Manhattan. Brooklyn, Queens, the Bronx, and Staten Island all grew more than twice as fast as the city's fanciest borough. And that population explosion has translated into development and dollars: in 2004, Brooklyn, Queens, and the Bronx each boasted more apartments under construction than Manhattan, according to plans filed with the city's Buildings Department. The value of this development: $1.6 billion. For the foreseeable future, 90 percent of the city's population growth is expected to be in the outer boroughs.

"The population in the late 1960s and 1970s had really declined," says Jonathan Bowles, head of the Center for an Urban Future, a local think tank.

"Storefronts were empty and in many cases it was dangerous to walk around. The immigrants really helped turn that around. Today there's no abandonment. The biggest problem facing many of these neighborhoods today is congestion." (To be fair, this is no minor issue. Overcrowded schools and overstressed infrastructure are severe problems that fall most heavily on immigrant families.)

Though we have created a rosy picture of the immigration boom of a hundred years back, the reality was far from ideal. When my grandfather came to New York, the idea of a city of immigrants scared long-term residents. Many, including reform-minded progressives like Jacob Riis, saw new arrivals as a criminal class. Despite immigrants' continued willingness to work long hours in difficult conditions for incredibly low pay, similar sentiments abound today. The first rumblings of discontent are being felt in the suburbs. Upscale Westchester County, for instance, has seen its immigrant population double over the last thirty years. And the influx has created tensions.

Take Brewster, New York, which has attracted a large pool of laborers, many of them Mexican, who regularly congregate on Main Street seeking daywork. In October 2005, when authorities discovered one of those Mexicans dead drunk and passed out behind a local school, the community responded with the kind of anger normally reserved for violent crimes. Rather than looking for ways to help the immigrants avoid social pathologies—such as creating a local hiring hall that would get the immigrants off the streets and ensure that these laborers are treated fairly by their employers—more than one hundred parents packed a school board meeting to push local legislators to lobby in Washington for tougher immigration laws. Similar protests have taken place in communities on Long Island.

But contrary to these concerns, there's evidence that immigrants actually make the city and its surroundings safer. Back in the 1960s, when New York's immigrant population plunged by more than 120,000, crime became rampant. By the end of the decade, the percentage of immigrants fell to 18 percent of the city's population, down from more than 41 percent in 1910.

The 1970s saw a small rebound in immigration but not enough to reverse the city's energy drain. Again, crime got worse. Immigration began its sustained rise in the 1980s, when an average of 85,000 people from abroad arrived each year. The annual number of immigrants flowing into New York increased 25 percent in the 1990s, to 104,000 people each year. And that's when crime began to fall.

Ramparsad's neighborhood provides a perfect example. White people fled the neighborhood in the 1990s (Cypress Hills' white population fell by 42.4 percent during the decade, according to the 2000 census and the City Planning Department statistics) and were replaced by such a swarm of new immigrants that the community's total population swelled by more than 7 percent despite the white flight. Those new arrivals, though poor (29 percent of the people in Cypress Hills live in poverty, according to the census), opened eighty-seven new businesses between 1998 and 2003, almost all of them mom-and-pop operations.

And what happened to crime during the same period? Reports from the New York City Police Department's CompStat Unit tell the story. In 1990, the Seventy-fifth precinct, which covers Cypress Hills, recorded 109 murders, 133 rapes, and 3,452 robberies. By 1998, just before Ramparsad arrived, there were 41 murders, 112 rapes, and 1,628 robberies. In 2005 (the latest statistics available run through December 18th), there were just 29 murders, 51 rapes, and 725 robberies. In the years since Ramparsad arrived in New York, murders dropped by 30 percent, rapes by 55 percent, and robberies by 56 percent. The NYPD reports similar declines in neighborhoods all over the city.

Though crime is likely a cyclical phenomenon (this would explain why much of the nation has also experienced a decline in violent crime over the past few years), and the NYPD's move toward community policing and zero tolerance for minor misbehavior has also had a hand in the reduction in violence, it's impossible to dismiss the notion that immigrants also influenced the trend.

"It didn't happen because of immigration alone, but it is one of the contributing factors," says Hiram Monserrate, a former police officer who now represents Corona, Jackson Heights, and Woodside, Queens, on New York's City Council. "Clearly, where there's more economic activity and more economic opportunity, there's less crime."

Irwine G. Clare, an immigrant rights advocate whose firm, Caribbean Immigrant Services, is based in Jamaica, Queens, adds: "We're here out of choice—and with choice comes responsibility and sacrifice. When people work, when they own things, when they are entrepreneurs, there is a tendency for crime to go down. New York is a good place to come and study, to come and work. It is not a good place to come and hustle."

Of course, you could argue that Ramparsad had it easy in New York City. Coming from an English-speaking Caribbean country, he had an advantage in being able to negotiate the system without having to learn a new tongue. Indeed, Ramparsad now has a green card, which entitles him to be here legally, and hopes eventually to become a citizen.

Perhaps Angela Diaz is more typical. She came to the United States at almost the same time as Ramparsad, from her native Colombia. She arrived at age nineteen, along with her mother and her aunt, all three of them clutching tourist visas entitling them to be in the United States for six months. And all three have stayed put, in violation of their visas, setting down roots in the borough of Queens, where they share an apartment. Diaz works in a gift shop in Corona, her mom is a home-health-care worker, and her aunt is a housekeeper who lives with a family on Long Island.

Despite the hardship of not being able to speak English when she arrived (in her first job, at a pizzeria in a mall on Long Island, customers routinely yelled at her and told her to go back to her country), Diaz says things are much tougher now. "At the beginning, no, I wasn't scared. But now it's scary, because I don't have papers." Diaz and her mother fear that they will be caught and deported.

What's more, though her command of English is now quite good, without papers Diaz cannot qualify for financial aid for higher education. And she is afraid that, simply by applying to City University, she will put herself, her mother, and her aunt on the radar of the Immigration and Naturalization Service (INS).

"I want to go to school, and I can't," she says. "I want another job, but I can't. I need papers to try to go to college. That's my dream, and I can't."

Queens Councilman Monserrate, for one, says Diaz and her family are right to be cautious. "Deportations are at an all-time high," the councilman says. "But, under the guise of September 11 and homeland security and antiterror efforts, the number-one group of deportees is Latinos. Isn't that interesting?" Indeed, the INS has been folded into the Department of Homeland Security, sending a not-so-subtle message to immigrants: we're in business to keep the United States safe and pure, not to welcome the huddled masses.

Diaz would plan for a future in New York if she could establish herself legally. Instead, she is sending her savings to Colombia to buy an apartment there in case she is deported.

"Colombia was better," she says of her six years in New York. "This city is just too much thinking and nothing in the heart. I thought that everything was going to be easy. But it's very hard. It's hard to be an immigrant. But we need jobs. That's why we're here."

Irwine Clare, the immigration advocate, suggests that the country must consider new strategies to help people like Diaz to earn legal status after they arrive. With so many immigrants working in the underground economy—waiting on street corners for low-wage construction work, earning under the table as home-health-care assistants, lining up in the mornings for work cleaning homes and offices—Clare sees the need for what he calls "earned legalization," a formal process in which people who overstayed their visas or arrived in the United States illegally can gain legal status by demonstrating that they have been productive citizens. Without that, he says, "we say to people, 'Don't travel.'"

Clare also calls for smart borders, not closed borders, for reasonable and quick review of immigration petitions (it takes twelve years for the INS to review petitions from legal residents to allow their brothers or sisters into the country, he says.) And he suggests that long-term residents, even if they are illegal, must be given an opportunity to change their immigration status. The waiting room of his office on the second floor of a little run-down building in Jamaica, Queens, is often full of people who have lived in New York for decades, whose children were born here and are American citizens, but who are forced to work at low wages in the subterranean economy because they're afraid of being deported.

But Clare doesn't see too many bright signs on the policy horizon. Moves like Real ID, a federal law that would deny immigrants the right to get drivers' licenses if they are here illegally or have violated the terms of their legal visas, show immigrants that they are no longer welcome in the United States. "As an immigrant, you're worse than an ax murderer."

The difficulty, says Gouri Sadhwani, executive director of the New York Civic Participation Project, a union-funded immigrant-rights organization, is that in the post-9/11 world, politicians have pushed Americans to be afraid of immigrants. "The right wing has done a very good job of trying to equate immigrants with terrorists," she says. "New immigrants today are more brown than they are white, and that is what the real debate is about, though nobody wants to talk about it."

Clare suggests that immigrants must get involved in politics if they are to change the terms of the debate. "I'm a national of Jamaica," he says with a smile. "I did not come to the United States for the sun, sea, or sand. I came here to better myself. In bettering myself, I contribute to the economic, social, and political fabric of my community." But, he adds, "although we throw the biggest party in North America [the West Indian Parade down Brooklyn's Eastern Parkway on Labor Day], although we have a large number of people who attend church, we have not translated that into benefits for our community. We party and we pray, but we don't politick well."

Still, the move into politics may take some time. As an El train screeches inbound from Crescent onto Fulton, Ramparsad confides that though he speaks English fluently, plans to become a citizen, and would like to buy the store where he works so he can invest his own money in growing the business, he takes no position on local or national political issues. "I don't mess with politics and religion," he says. "That's too much fuss, too much argument, too much nothing."

Even so, if current trends continue, he may have to break his vow. In neighborhoods all over the city, including Cypress Hills, immigrants are becoming victims of their own success. Housing prices are rising (a recent survey by the National Low Income Housing Coalition suggested that a person would have to work 132 hours a week in a minimum wage job to be able to afford a market-rent two-bedroom apartment in the city). But instead of being satisfied, landlords are increasingly looking to rip off new immigrants by charging even higher prices, rather than rent to more experienced residents who know what comparable costs are in their communities. Along the main drags in Corona, not far from where Diaz works, many For Rent flyers taped to local lampposts no longer indicate how many rooms an apartment has; instead, they note how many people the landlord will allow in the apartment—an indication that property owners want to capitalize on new immigrants who are willing to band together and live in overcrowded conditions in order to make their way in the city. What's more, in places like Washington Heights, which has long been an immigrant neighborhood, old timers are finding that their kids are being forced out of the city by the high cost of housing. This ramp-up in rents and housing prices may have a devastating affect on New York's ability to continue to attract immigrants in the future.

And this, in turn, will have a devastating impact on the city. For immigrants, whether legal or illegal, are key to the future of New York. Without its immigrants, the city would continue to shrink. Without perpetual new arrivals from abroad to replenish the population, New York City would lose its vibrant culture and much of its economic base. Immigrants may need New York, but New York needs immigrants more.

Says Sadhwani, herself an immigrant from Shillong, India: "We need to be able to show new immigrants that power, whether economic, political or social, is theirs to have. The argument is that immigrants will alter our democracy. And, yes, they will—but in a good way."

Notes

1. These and many of the statistics in this essay are culled from Rae Rosen, Susan Wieler, and Joseph Pereira, *New York City Immigrants: The 1990s Wave* 11, no. 6 (June 2005); New York City Department of City Planning, *The Newest New Yorkers, 2000*, October 2004.
2. This trend is documented in Jeffrey S. Passel and Roberto Suro, Pew Hispanic Center, Washington, D.C., *Rise, Peak, and Decline: Trends in U.S. Immigration, 1992–2004*, September 27, 2005.

EXTINCTION

Katrina Lenček-Inagaki

We called it the "Baby Park." Officially, the 1.6 acres of Lower Manhattan was called Washington Market Park, but everyone in the neighborhood knew what you were talking about when you mentioned the Baby Park. With its simple wood and red-metal playground, patchy lawn, community garden, and dilapidated gazebo, the park may not have offered much for "big kids," but it was a paradise for younger children. Warm weather meant cavorting in the sprinkler (my older brother Misko quickly learned to manipulate the height of the spurting water by plugging certain sprinkler holes), birthday parties in the gazebo, and children selling various goods outside the park's black wrought-iron fence. We set up a lemonade stand in front of the Baby Park once, but it wasn't very profitable, and our mother had to console us with ice cream bars—a gumball-eyed clown bar for me and a Mickey Mouse one for my brother. I remember it all so vividly: the big white ice cream truck outside the entrance, the pain of getting splinters from the rough wooden playground equipment, the joy of running across the swinging wood-and-chain suspension bridge that led to the slide and the slide into the sand. I remember the Baby Park the way it was fourteen years ago when I started as a kindergartner at P.S.234 across the street from it. But in the spring of 2002, all the old equipment was removed, and $1 million worth of shiny equipment has since replaced the ramshackle setup. Just the other day, I walked past the park. How alien it looked! The sophisticated new playground with its "airy, minimalist" play ship, the beige and gray striped safety surface decorated with yellow circles. The small garden plots once cheaply rented to neighborhood families are now a single, company-sponsored Children's Garden. These days, the park is far more crowded, filled with kids mostly with their nannies (parents evidently went the way of the old equipment). And as for sidewalk sales, well, rich kids don't sit on the sidewalk selling junk now, do they? It is not just the playground that has been transformed, it is the entire neighborhood. What happened to the Triangle Below Canal? Thanks to gentrification, that home, that vibrant, dynamic, artistic community—the TriBeCa of my youth—no longer exists.

The refurbished Washington Market Park in TriBeCa adds a particularly suburban touch to this once-edgy but now-upscale neighborhood.

I know, I know, the area has been changing since before I was even born. Manhattan's trapezoidal Lower West Side area was not even called TriBeCa until the 1960s, when enterprising developers coined the catchy name. I grew up among history's leftovers: crumbling brick buildings with wide canopies, old warehouses, and rusted metal storefront signs such as Warren Street's United Rubber Co. Even my loft's big windows with their low sills, an architectural feature characteristic of TriBeCa, are left over from the days when workmen passed crates of dairy products through them. For, once upon a time in the late 1800s, TriBeCa was New York City's wholesale dairy district. The district, known then as the Washington Market, soon expanded beyond butter and eggs (interestingly, Butter and Eggs is the name of an overpriced furniture store a few blocks from my house), and by the 1930s, the wholesale markets of the Lower West Side had become the world's largest, selling sardines from Norway, venison and bear steaks, 7.5 million cases of eggs, and 4.5 million tubs of butter, as well as other nonfood items as diverse as pets, radios, garden seeds, textiles, and church supplies.[1] But as the 1950s progressed, the industry began to rely less on horse-drawn carriages and more on big trucks. Huge vehicles were not compatible with TriBeCa's narrow, ancient streets, and this transportation difficulty combined with economic changes—the shift of trade businesses out of New York City and the Washington Street Urban Renewal project—spelled trouble for the Lower West Side wholesale district.

Bad news for the manufacturing and selling firms; good news for city artists, who by the mid-1970s were already starting to be priced out of SoHo. TriBeCa's industrial spaces offered the high ceilings, profuse natural light, and inexpensive cost ideal for artists, especially those working in the large-scale format popular at the time. These lofts, not yet legally converted for residential use, were so desired that artists moved into them anyway.

Although not among this illegal wave of colonizers, my artist parents were pioneers when they moved into TriBeCa in 1982. During my early childhood, all basic amenities, such as the supermarket, veterinarian, and Laundromat, were in SoHo. TriBeCa was empty and quiet. It was common for kids to play catch in the street. I learned to ride a bicycle in a parking lot. The area was still transitioning out of wholesaling goods, and according to my mother, I used to love looking at the fish tanks at nearby Petrosino Fish Market. That fish market is gone now, and though I do not remember it, I do remember the Pennsylvania Pretzel Company, Job Lot, Hamburger Harry's, Downtown Cottage, Woolworth's, Ray's Pizza, and the comic book store on Chambers Street. And most of all, Nolan's Deli, right across Greenwich Street from P.S.234. A thin layer of dust covered the entire place, kids with Jansport backpacks jostled to buy Sour Power candy by the piece, and the deli man sold *Penthouse* to fifth-grade boys. Gone. All those restaurants, all those stores, gone. I can still remember mailing letters at the stately, century-old Prince Street Post Office—now the proud home of Apple's flagship New York store. Though it's hard to tell now, SoHo wasn't always Downtown's answer to Madison Avenue.

But back then, no frills meant residents were a self-selecting group. My mother, a visual artist and active TriBeCa resident, says, "as an artist you want a certain environment that allows for creative freedom. Grunginess feeds creativity. You don't see, you don't want. In TriBeCa you could go out looking tough and kind of disappear into the scruffiness of the neighborhood." Today, dry cleaners, pediatricians, video stores, preschool programs, buildings with doormen, expensive restaurants (Robert De Niro's Tribeca Grill opened in 1990, Nobu in 1994), and antique stores abound. Rising rents have ushered in pricey boutiques and big chain stores like Starbucks. Plans for a Whole Foods are in development, and in the past two years, there has been an absurd proliferation of gyms. Gyms!

In 2004, according to the Corcoran Group, the average TriBeCa condo sold for $924,000, the average loft $1.49 million. Real estate reports including Citi Habitats' Black and White Report have cited SoHo/TriBeCa as the most expensive place to live in the city. Most painters, sculptors, dancers, and writers do not have the kind of income necessary to secure a loan for a multimillion dollar home. But for the nouveau TriBeCans, money is no object. Between 1980 and 2000, TriBeCa's population boomed by the tens of thousands; the U.S. Census reported TriBeCa and Battery Park City's combined population to be 15,918 in 1980, 34,420 in 2000. And the population has grown sharply since then, thanks in part to the government's aggressive post 9/11 development programs in Lower Manhattan. The new residents come with different expectations. They are not seeking quiet artistic refuge, they want an investment and the "neighborhood experience." My mother remembers that back in the day,

> everybody shared the venture of pioneering, of getting into a building that was a warehouse or a manufacturing building with freight elevators, exposed brick walls, rattling windows, and stairs that weren't fireproof. They took what was there and made the best of it, trying to fix the space up so they could live and work in it. And then when they had children they would break up the loft spaces into working and living spaces.

The bond, the shared understanding between TriBeCa's first residents, remains strong today, even though they no longer dominate the neighborhood.

My brother and I were part of the first generation of TriBeCa-born children, and all my playmates' parents were neighborhood artists. I recently visited the New Museum's exhibit on the 1980's art scene, East Village USA, and I saw work by three of my childhood friends' parents: a sculptor, a video artist, and a musician. TriBeCa provided these artists with an environment to create successful work, but you did not need to be an established artist to live there. As a consequence, we, their children, grew up in an environment of genuine creative struggle, grew up in a very specific and, in some ways, idyllic fashion. We were encouraged in our individuality, progressively schooled, and blissfully unaware of the material culture that so pervaded uptown elementary schools. (When I entered the Upper East Side–school Spence as a ninth grader, I was shocked to see first graders with highlighted hair, wearing pink UGGS.) There were so few of us that we all knew each other, and, in true TriBeCa fashion, I had several multiracial friends (like me!) at a time when interracial dating was still a social faux pas.

I wonder if the banker and glitterati residents realize that they are not only ruining the open and villagelike environment of my youth by formalizing everything but also sabotaging themselves by moving into high-rises and overcrowding the schools. Locals used to call TriBeCa "sky country," but the open vistas are quickly disappearing as demand for living space increases. The government plays a significant role in this particular aspect of TriBeCa's gentrification—more than $800 million worth of Liberty Bonds were issued to development companies to build massive residences like the currently underway twenty-four-story, 274-unit Tribeca Green on Warren Street and North End Avenue. The government has a vested interest in developing areas, rehabilitating them, and gentrifying them for economic gain. Not only do rich neighborhoods equal lots of tax dollars for the municipal government, but businesses are good for the economy...artists in warehouses are not. So while the influx of business types (including entertainment-industry executives) does contribute to gentrification, the government is partially to blame for the gentrification as well. After all, the government paid for the creation of the luxury condos in order to lure a specific kind of resident. In the past eight years, gigantic residences such as The Solaire at 20 River Terrace have popped up in Battery Park City, blocking the view from my father's TriBeCa apartment. We used to be able to see the whole river from my father's balcony on Greenwich Street, but now we are left with a tiny sliver peeking between "full-service" buildings with indoor pools, children's playrooms, and garages. I want my view back! I do suppose there is some consolation to be had—20 River Terrace is the United States's first environmentally advanced residential building. And thanks to multilevel humidification and ventilation systems that supply filtered fresh air to each residential unit,[2] the building residents needn't breathe the neighborhood air. I hope our air is okay, because I have been breathing it for eighteen years.

My family owns our loft, so I know I won't be pushed out of TriBeCa. But what I wonder is whether I'll even want to live there.

Notes

1. B. Stewart, "What 80 Warren Street Knows," *New York Times*, August 11, 2002, 1.
2. "River Terrace—The Solaire," *American Institute of Architects*, April 22, 2004, http://www.aiatopten.org/hpb/overview.cfm?ProjectID=273 (accessed June 4, 2005).

THE GREAT MALL OF NEW YORK

Michael Sorkin

All cities laminate many models of spatial organization and use. Inscribed within New York are fragments of medieval, Georgian, industrial, suburban, modernist, City Beautiful, and other urban patterns that, meeting the grid and its exceptions, coalesce to ground the contemporary city. These spatial arrangements are activated by an even greater range of styles of use and inhabitation that power New York's dynamism and self-transforming energy. A constant stream of immigrants—people and ideas—and their shifting habits and desires takes the physical defaults with which they are confronted and morphs them to accommodate their skills, ambitions, and need for the familiar. The market—whether the speculative gyre of real estate that drives so much of the local economy, the long-wave shift from production to service employment, or the growing dominance of globalized retail operations that increasingly mark every city—subject New York to constant revision to accommodate the insatiable needs of capital.

Is the city growing suburban? Perhaps. But searching for the evidence requires some sense of what it means to be suburban and clearly demands proof beyond the odd McMansion in Queens or shopping mall in Manhattan—the city has always thrived on anomaly. Widespread anxiety about suburbanization suggests bigger fears that some annihilating principle threatens to sweep across our protective rivers and torque the thick and sociable city—with its sacred architectures and comforting rituals—into something we no longer recognize. This portrait of the city at risk presupposes a particular idea of suburbanism. These suburbs are not the symbiotic dependencies of the street-car era nor the genteel Ardens in Westchester and Fairfield that continue to serve as ruling class dormitories, points on the power triangle of Yale, Wall Street, and New Canaan. Nor is the threatening suburbia that of the deteriorating "inner ring," a zone lapsing

Unlike its suburban counterparts, there is no parking lot at Home Depot's first Manhattan store, opened in 2004 on Twenty-third Street between Sixth and Seventh avenues. Customers must wheel away purchases in their own carts.

113

into a syndrome long associated with the city itself: the complex of unemployment, drug use, bad schools, collapsing infrastructure, and failing public facilities—everything the middle class once fled the city to escape.

Rather, these dangerous suburbs are more recent, part of a toxic compound of spatial and cultural forces that afflict all the space of the contemporary environment. These suburbs originated in the postwar years, the result of the most deliberate project of national redesign since the imposition of the Jeffersonian grid. Like that universalizing instrument, postwar suburbia has been a force for homogeneity masquerading as choice. In the endlessly (but trivially) recombinant brandscape that has become America's emblematic pattern of settlement, daily life is designed to maximize consumption—of goods, of time, of energy, of processed information. And so we produce the sprawl of Orange County or Atlanta, those nightmare worlds of super-sized houses, super-sized cars, super-sized people, super-sized habits of getting and spending. Lurking darkly in the ideological background is the panoply of secular humanist anxieties, the Republicanism, the religiosity, the tightly bound psychopathologies that produce Columbine, Jon Benet Ramsey, and the bland violence of the American nightmare. Bush country.

What are the origins of this suspect place? The instruments that created and organized this sprawling territory were spatial, financial, and ethical. The paradigm of the individual house in an individual yard on a street of identical yards and houses was multiply ingrained in the culture. The fantasy of ownership, historic marker of enfranchised citizenship and traditional home of the American dream, became postwar policy via the easy availability of FHA loans to (white) veterans, accelerated depreciation for suburban businesses, gigantic subsidies for infrastructure (led by the vast project to construct the interstates, their cloverleaf access points managing suburban space with the precision of the mile grid), and by the Manichaean counterpoise of city and suburb with greenfield rancheros for the anointed classes and urban renewal public housing complexes for the noisome, miscolored poor.

These suburbs were also the operating system for the radically reconfigured style of consumption that now dominates world culture. In the postwar suburb, everything to be had was taken into the realm of mass consumption, remodeled as a consumer good, rolled out with the maniacal replicability of our wartime production of the arsenal of democracy—cars replacing tanks, split-levels for high altitude bombers. The animating, transitional object was the automobile, the key for unlocking the system as a whole: the suburbs simply could not be inhabited without a car at each domestic unit's disposal, and the automobile was the touchstone of the "what's good for General Motors" mentality that had—since the high Fordist era—ratcheted up the scale and intensity of the social necessity of things. The need for multiple cars, the meaningless, style-driven, keeping-up-with-the-Joneses incitements to trade in last year's for this year's version, and the willful profligacy of gas-guzzling, long-distance driving created a sector of expenditure that represented a new and habituating idea of consumer necessity.

The automobile system permitted and modeled a similar mass-market approach to spatial products. Here, the paradigms are Levittown, the strip, and the shopping mall. The ticky-tacky, all-look-the-same boxes of sprawling suburbs were simply real estate iterations of production and marketing techniques perfected in the automobile industry. The same superficial inflections of difference, the same segmentations of the market with its pressure to constantly move up, the same potlatch of energy and spatial consumption, the same branded aura, and the same predication in and reinforcement of the nuclear family and woman-at-home lifestyles moved both products and linked them inextricably. Where once mobility had been a leveler—a social encounter on foot or in a streetcar—movement now atomized, accelerating the podification of the American subject, isolated in a 2,000-pound prosthesis, breathing refreshed air, radio on.

Of course, the big ticket items could only function via a logistics chain that constantly replenished, repaired, maintained, and improved them. This produced two characteristic sites of consumption, the strip and the mall, both of which grew from precedented formats, greatly attenuated by their adaptation to automotive culture. The strip was the logical scaling up of Main Street to accommodate the speed and habits of shoppers in cars, calibrated to quick in-and-out trips for gas, groceries, fast food. The mall—from its initial incarnation as shopping center to its apotheosis in the universal big box of Wal Mart—offered a centralized, park-once, shop-many-times format that—like hub-and-spoke air transit—offered the icy dogmatism of an efficient diagram. In both of these formats, the epistemological glue was provided by the brand, whether in the institutional semiotics of Kmart, Costco, Esso, McDonald's, Taco Bell, or Chuck E. Cheese's, or in the universally branded (and bar-coded) goods on offer within—Tide, Crest, Green Giant, Cheerios, Martha, Calvin, Nike, Panasonic, Sony—with their endlessly disciplined uniformity and "quality." This suburban mode of consumption was driven by the endless transfer in an infinite stream of Chevys, Buicks, Hondas, and Fords of branded goods from these centralized emporia to the waiting closets, freezers, walls, and garages of home, the penultimate link on the global logistics chain that end in Alpine landfills.

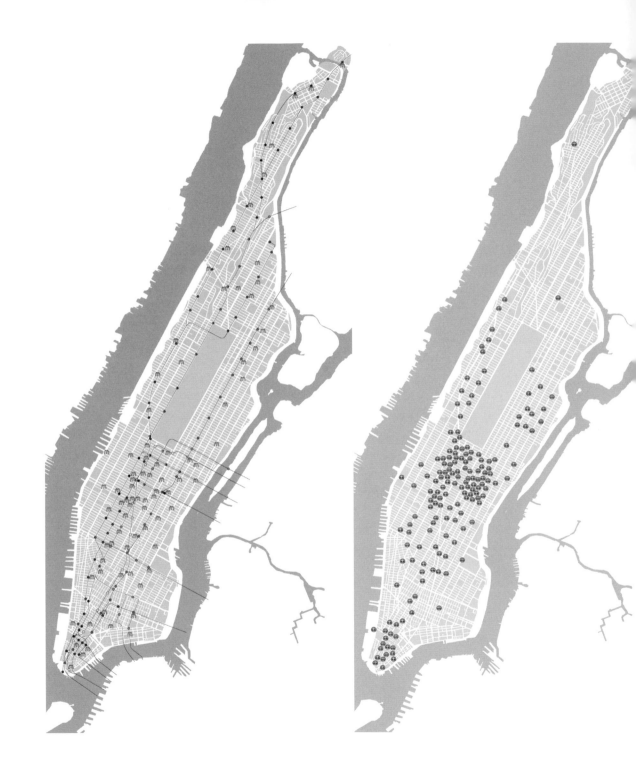

New Yorkers are not exactly slouches in the consumption department, and we are, like many suburbanites, crippled and confined by a distorted economics of habitat. For many in the city, however, the suburban horizon continues to reflect a dream world of spacious houses, clean streets, and cheap shopping. Indeed, surprising numbers of the city's poorest citizens make their way—by carpool and bus—to outlying malls to enjoy their low prices, disciplined sociability, and one-stop convenience. While city policy continues to vigorously resist the construction of big-box stores within residential and commercial neighborhoods, the debate over their benefits is in no way resolved. Questions of displacement of local businesses, of traffic generation, of out-of-scale building, of the hegemony of the corporate way of doing business, of upstream consequences for workers in sweatshops abroad affect cities and suburbs alike. Many New Yorkers take comfort in the apparent fact that these places have yet to arrive in serious numbers, at least not in their originary suburban form.

And yet they have found their own way in. The city has been infused with a nearly ubiquitous infrastructure of multinational commerce that has, to a remarkable degree, fitted itself to existing commercial settings, spatial scales, and ethnic and class organization. Like the suburbs, we are awash in McDonald's, Starbucks, Gaps, Staples, Old Navys, Blockbusters, KFCs, Toys "R" Us, and other familiar multinational retailers. Indeed, our native retailers—from Bloomingdale's to Barnes & Noble—are themselves now part of the portfolios of corporations larger still. Far from proving resistant to this commercial rationalization, the city has been penetrated by a commercialization process enabled by historic spatial formats that have proved remarkably adaptable and by a real estate market that constantly ratchets prices upward, creating a legendarily hostile environment for small and low-margin businesses in general. The issue for the city is, thus, whether the literal content of these places is so inimical to traditional urban styles of commerce and sociability that the city is itself transformed in some fundamental and irreversible way. The picture in Manhattan is not promising, as the following cases suggest.

Finding Fast Food

The locational formula for fast-food outlets is constant for cities and suburbs: traffic. Just as suburban McDonald's franchises are attracted to strips, malls, and highway interchanges, their urban relations are closely correlated with subway stations and high-volume institutions. Reflecting the station density of the subway itself, this leads to a predictable clumping in business and shopping districts. There is, however, an egalitarian quality to the borough-wide pattern,

opposite
LEFT:
Fast (Food) Track
RIGHT:
The Starbucks
Archipelago

with a relatively evenly spaced distribution of outlets in the poorer neighborhoods of upper Manhattan. While consumption behavior may vary according to income and other social factors, the locational pattern in Manhattan does not correlate with either poverty or obesity. The ubiquity of these outlets reflects a more crucial pervasiveness: the universal presence of television, the main instrument for the incitement of structured consumption. Television is the too-little-acknowledged enabler of suburban life, a cultural point source that paradoxically immobilizes leisure activity in couch-potato mode while, at the same time, converting it to a school for the more energetic pattern of a daily life focused on shopping. Television is the great elider of city and suburb, creating spatial equivalence for every living room and priming the shopping reflex to be activated by remorselessly encoded signals. Have it your way. Freedom of choice. At McDonald's.

The Starbucks Archipelago

The distribution—and numbers—of Starbucks correspond closely to the pattern established by McDonald's. There is a close relationship between Starbucks and subway stations and the same attraction to major institutional locations—hospitals, universities, etc. However, there is a dramatic absence of Starbucks in northern Manhattan, with only four locations north of 110th Street (two of these adjoin Columbia University). Unlike McDonald's, Starbucks is a close predictor of neighborhood income. The chain-cafe phenomenon is not exactly a fresh intrusion: although product and price point differ, Starbucks joins a historic pattern—notably the Chock full o'Nuts brand—that has legs as an urban phenomenon. Unlike its aggressive down-market competitor—Dunkin' Donuts—Starbucks represents more than a necessary jolt of caffeine stimulation; it carries an aura of "lifestyle," an invidious prepackaged formula of self-authentication. Part of the genius of the Starbucks brand is its suburbanization of a quintessentially urban phenomenon—the coffee house—and its reinscription in the city as a generic, branded commodity. While I am agnostic about the product, the distribution of Starbucks maps the push of uniformity and the fetish of universal commodities that represents the suburbanization of everything.

The 125th Street Mall

The main street of Harlem and, by extension, of African America, is 125th Street. It is the historic home of cultural institutions like the Apollo Theater and the Studio Museum and has long held a mix of small shops and street vendors aimed at a local clientele. Over the years, control of commerce on 125th Street by

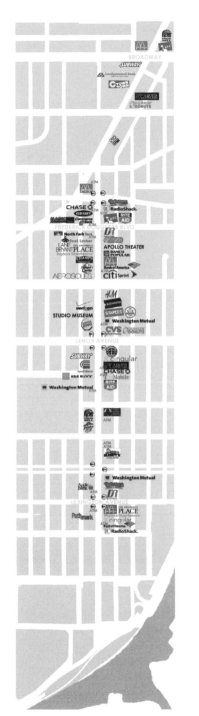

LEFT:
125th Street
RIGHT:
Vegas Fifth Avenue

119 *The Great Mall of New York*

white and Asian non-neighborhood owners has been the subject of considerable contention—even violence. Today, the situation has changed dramatically. As gentrification of Harlem proceeds at a rapid clip, the character of 125th Street has itself been transformed, marked by the brisk penetration by multinational chains. Indeed, 125th Street has, effectively, become the urban analogue to a suburban mall, cleansed of locality. Anchored at one end by a multiplex theater in a building that also houses several national chain stores and at the other by a major supermarket (a considerable rarity in Manhattan), the street's once singular, if frayed, character is rapidly tipping into the generic. The politics of this transformation are vexed.

While the global chains are an even more incendiary accelerant for the departure of local shops, driving out small-scale retailers and sending real estate prices skyrocketing, they also constitute a form of acknowledgment for a community long ghettoized and neglected, a kind of welcome into a larger community. The complicated relationship between brand and identity—which plagues us all—has, as is widely noted, become ingrained in the consumption habits of African American youth. While this is not the place to deconstruct the importance of Tommy Hilfiger and Nike to the self-definition and social currency of this community, it is clear that this is a decidedly suburban phenomenon, part of a more general convergence of national values of aspirational consumption. As can be seen all over the city, the shopping mall—which has the street as its prototype—simply readapts itself to its originating source. With subway stops in the position of mall entrances, 125th Street is seamlessly initiated into the multinational system.

Vegas Fifth Avenue

A much-observed marketing trend is the emergence of "experience retail," which amounts to the merger of shopping and entertainment in explicit, "themed" fashion. Themed retail is a strategy for extending the authority of the brand by taking its meanings into ever more diffuse territories of association, a displacement of object by aura. The origins of experience retail are complex but can certainly be associated, in the near term, with the creative imaginative geography of the theme park and, in the longer term, with the rise of the larger social category of luxury within the context of the mobile aspirations of bourgeois culture. Much of midtown Manhattan—the experiential ground zero for New York tourism—has been co-opted as the locus for a set of "destination" stores that might be found in Las Vegas, Orlando, or Dubai. These include the Disney Store, the Warner Brothers Store, the NBA Store, the NBC Store, the Museum of Modern

Art Store, the Metropolitan Museum Store, and Planet Hollywood, as well as a plethora of high-end retail chains.

The local genius of cities lies in its marshaling of a wide diversity of experiences and in the particular patterns with which these experiences are deployed. Every city represents a compendium of places, and the pleasure of the city lies in both the special qualities of neighborhoods and in the circulation between their differences. The mosaic of New York has long been a particularly dynamic and variegated instance of the energy of difference and the array of its distinctive places—Harlem, Chinatown, Little Italy, Greenwich Village, the Lower East Side, Atlantic Avenue, Flushing, etc.—and has derived from self-organizing aspects of each of these localities and their embodiment of the cultural communities that make up the city. They remain, nevertheless, distinctly of New York, inhabiting a range of physical space and architectural types that are specific to the city, adapting imported cultural patterns to native spatial typologies.

If suburbanization—or globalization—threatens the city, the main danger comes not from the physical side of the equation, the introduction of specific alien architectures from suburbia—big boxes, ranch houses, shopping malls, etc.—but from the content side, which has proven adaptable enough to remain relatively independent of the constraints of its setting. To be sure, Trump Tower and the Time Warner Center are interiorized malls but are not effectively different from traditional urban department stores, themselves frequently organized into a series of designer boutiques. The issue, rather, is the uniformity of content—the same Sephora, Armani, Victoria's Secret, Sharper Image, and Talbot's as anywhere else on the planet.

Incredible amounts of ink have been expended—pro and con—on the transformation of Times Square into a corporate amusement park, particularly the concessionary arrangement that made a once-raunchy block of Forty-second Street into a Disney fiefdom awash with franchised fun. Here is the Disney effect succinctly achieved. As at the Disneylands themselves, each entered through a generic "Main Street" housing a variety of multinational establishments, the trick is to house an identical content behind a hollow locality. Thus Fifth Avenue—the city's premier retail address—remains stately, and Forty-second Street glitters with neon extravagance, even as each is stripped of its meaningful particulars. Delocalized in content, Manhattan's sites are free for promiscuous global recombination, to reappear in Beijing or Vegas or L.A. or anywhere. It isn't that the city is becoming *physically* suburban, simply that it's becoming the same as everyplace else.

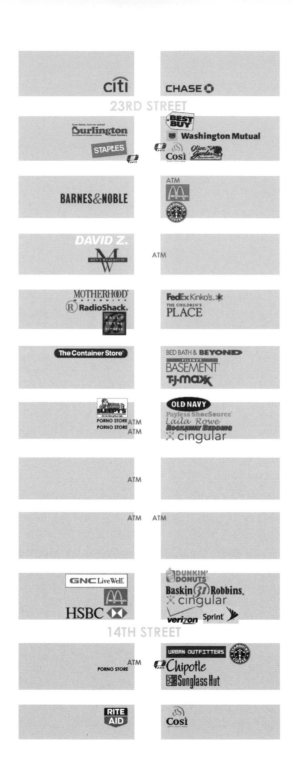

The Return of the Ladies Mile

By the years following the Civil War—the blocks of Broadway from Fourteenth Street to Twenty-third Street—had come to be the city's premier high-end shopping district, known as the "Ladies Mile," a predecessor of Fifth Avenue's current status. Enabled by the invention of the "safe" space of the department store, by a solidified middle class and its creation of women's leisure and the shifting mores that offered it greater independence, New York underwent a shopping revolution. The result was this tight district, continuously lined by department stores and other dry-goods shops. This district was itself mobile, having been first established farther downtown and later migrating to Midtown, reflecting both the northward movement of population and the energetic real estate speculation that has always been the core driver of spatial location in the city.

Toward the end of the century, as department stores first reached their maximum scale and as an elevated rail line was constructed on Sixth Avenue, a second retail spine grew to the west of Ladies Mile, also between Fourteenth to Twenty-third streets. It was lined with enormous, marvelously designed department stores, many a full block long, and the growth of this complex paralleled a decline in the Ladies Mile—squeezed out by the development of skyscraper office buildings, the presence of sweatshops with their "unfashionable" workers, the continued northern migration of the upper classes, and the competition from the dramatic growth of retail into ever larger establishments. A similar fate was to befall the department stores of Sixth Avenue, in turn, as the major emporia—like Macy's, Altman's, and Lord & Taylor—built new stores farther uptown.

Two protosuburban organizational patterns are clearly visible in this nineteenth-century story. The Ladies Mile was anchored at either end by Union Square and Madison Square, themselves surrounded by commercial activity. If the scale was greater, the dumbbell *parti* closely resembles the classic organization of the suburban shopping mall developed a century later: the idea of a back-and-forth circulation induced by strong magnets is mall design writ. Likewise, the finitude of classic shopping streets—in both their small town and big city incarnations—reflects the combined demands of patience, fatigue, and variety. Indeed, the parallel development of street-based shopping and its interiorized variant has been in play for centuries. Shopping malls *avant la lettre* are surely visible in the arcades of Paris, London, or Milan, in the souks of the Arab world, in covered market halls, and a variety of other architectural armatures.

Both the Ladies Mile and Sixth Avenue reflect an organization characteristic of suburban malls, their careful response to market segmentation. This division into up- and down-market malls, high- and low-rent shopping streets, and upscale

opposite
Ladies Mile

and downscale stores is a fact of shopping that transcends spatiality and adapts with ease to a wide variety of formats. Finally, the finite duration of the commercial lives of the Ladies Mile and its Sixth Avenue double have a comparable life in the suburbs. Witness current concerns with the proliferation of "dead malls" and the devastating comings and goings of Wal-Mart in the pursuit of superior locational demographics and better taxation and subsidy deals. The permanence of commercial arrangements is not a product of sentiment but of the bottom line.

In the past decade, the old department stores of Sixth Avenue—long considered dysfunctional for most contemporary uses—have undergone a remarkable revival. Preserved from demolition by landmarks designation, inefficient for conversion to residential use, and demandingly large, these buildings were long thought to be dinosaurs, immune to reuse. But then the suburbs arrived. In a short span of years, the district has been revived as a shopping nexus, now populated by the ranks of global retail—Bed, Bath, and Beyond, Old Navy, Barnes & Noble, Staples, Filene's Basement, the whole panoply of midrange mall stand-bys. Is this a sign of suburbanization or simply the return of a phenomenon of distinctly urban origin? Both, probably. Sixth Avenue is newly lively, packed with pedestrians, and this activity certainly helps local shops on adjacent streets, and the old department store spaces are again in use. Perhaps this is the best we can hope for.

There Goes the Neighborhood

My own block lies in the center of Greenwich Village, a quirky, historic bohemia, dense with students, tenaciously liberal, preservation obsessed, and scaled for intimacy and chance encounter. This romantic view, however, is belied by certain facts on the ground. I live near the West Fourth Street subway station—a major transfer point that runs like a grotty, detached, shopless mall under Sixth Avenue—ten blocks south of the reborn retail corridor described above. Like 125th Street, a thoroughfare that was once distinguished by the particulars of its locality, Sixth Avenue is now a strangely (contested) mix of multinational franchises and more local businesses. To be sure, it is not a local street but a highly trafficked north–south axis. Moreover, the Village remains an entertainment destination for a very wide variety of people and houses a huge number of students, a population of temporarily limited means.

The blocks of Sixth Avenue near me represent an extremely fluid intersection of a very wide variety of interests that range from the most distinct to the most generic, a vivid seam between suburban homogeneity and urban resistance. Here, I think, is encountered the most graphic and decisive difference between

There goes the neighborhood.

city and suburb: the influential presence of the street. The sometimes oppressive raffishness of this stretch of Sixth Avenue is secured by three particular presences that are decidedly problematic components of the suburban landscape: The first is a two-block row of sidewalk booksellers, mainly homeless black men, who offer used magazines and books from folding tables that line the sidewalk. The second is the regular presence of several political activists and advocates who distribute literature and raise funds from smaller tables. And the third is a garish row of sex shops and tattoo parlors clustered in another block.

The triple configuration of chains, local shops, and these "exceptional" activities operate in strange concert. The combination certainly serves as a curb to the gentility that abounds on many surrounding blocks via both its insistent diversity and its "dangerous" content. Despite the plethora of fast-food shops, cell-phone stores, and chain drugstores, this is a place that is not like the mall, with its rigorous exclusion of undesirables, its prohibitions of the exercise of free speech, and its G-rated content. Indeed, the attraction of this space with these marginalized activities can be seen as an urban coping mechanism, in which an array of powerful urban antigens is drawn to the site of multinational malignancy. And, once again, the unyielding spatial character of a neighborhood with strong preservation protections assures that the upward spiral of scale that characterizes so much suburban retail is frustrated. Once again, the inconvenience of the historic city becomes a bulwark for the protection of the very possibility of diversity and the local.

But if these porn stores and tattoo parlors help retain the louche credibility of the Village, they function as the theming elements that give this particular mall its distinction as a destination and "experience." Without a doubt, Sixth Avenue has been taken over by usual globalization, becoming a compendium of familiar brands inscribed in the yielding tissue of historic scales and architectures. Daily the tour buses roll by and visitors from Omaha or Toronto can point out the local Starbucks or Uno's Pizzeria, just like the one back home, only different somehow. If suburbia is all about packaging uniformity to create the limited and malleable differences of branding, then the suburbs are here.

Suburban Nation

I often have trouble sleeping and find myself sitting in the living room, reading or watching TV. In a dozen windows across the way, I can see the flicker of cathode tubes as students and insomniacs burn the midnight oil whether purposefully or desperately. If there is a growing reciprocity between suburban and urban patterns and behaviors, it is clearly mediated by the great equalizers of mass electronic media and by the commercial universalism of the Brand. While one worries about the destabilization of physical space under the regime of the virtual, this anxiety has diffuse results. In terms of the annihilating effects of suburban organization on great cities like New York, the risk seems only marginally formal. The city has been active and effective in defending its treasures of architecture and texture. But this defense has been dangerously narrow, a kind of neutron bomb of aesthetic consideration. We save the facades of our buildings but have little concern for their human content. This is not to slight the importance of maintaining physical continuity, respecting the achievements of past generations. However, as rampant gentrification, the elevation of shopping and mass entertainment to the center of cultural activity, and the triumph of branding and multinational economic arrangements become pervasive, the specific character of the city, with its ability to multiply differences, risks being reduced to an empty shell, the decorative experience that frames a life too uniform.

THE RISE OF REAL ESTATE AND THE DECLINE OF THE INDUSTRIAL CITY

Matthew Schuerman

In 1999, one of the country's best-known producers of kosher wine wanted to expand its Brooklyn distribution center into an abandoned brewery on the East River, right next to its old plant. The company, Royal Wine Company, which makes the Kedem and Baron Herzog brands, employed about sixty office and warehouse workers and expected to grow to one hundred employees. But the city, which had taken possession of the brewery after the Schaefer Brewing Company left town, begged off. It found other parcels for the wine company, and even offered some incentives, but none met Royal Wine's requirements.

The placement of signs such as these along Fifty-ninth Street promoting New York as The Real Estate Capital of the World unabashedly reveals the new mentality of a city for sale to the highest bidder.

The brewery property itself had been reserved, through a political deal, for apartments. The site was located on the border between Hasidic and Hispanic Williamsburg. The tension between the two groups was so great and the need for affordable apartments so intense that Hispanics had staged a sit-in six years earlier when a new public housing complex opened, protesting what they saw as an unfair tenant-selection process. The state assemblyman from the area, a Democrat named Vito Lopez, had crossed party lines to endorse Mayor Giuliani for re-election in 1997 after the mayor promised to consider the brewery site for low-income apartments. "There is such a demand for housing in Williamsburg," Lopez told the *New York Times*, "that affordable housing [should] be a priority over the retention of jobs."[1]

That indeed came to pass, though at considerable cost. The first units in a mixed-income development, called Schaefer Landing, opened on the site in late 2005. Once finished, the development will consist of two high-rise towers containing 210 luxury condominiums and 140 rent-controlled apartments for low-income people. The city and state paid $6.7 million for the environmental cleanup and will reimburse the developers with $38 million in cash and tax credits.[2] The condos have been selling quickly, fetching $640,000 to $1.9 million per unit.[3] Royal Wine and its one hundred jobs have moved to a 140,000-square-foot warehouse in Bayonne, New Jersey.

Industrial companies have been fighting residential—and commercial—development in New York City for fifty years, and they have been losing. The number of industrial sector jobs (including transportation, utilities, and construction employment) has dropped from 2 million to the current 500,000.[4] Traditional explanations for industry's decline point to automation and cheaper labor abroad. But that does not explain why manufacturing jobs, while declining within the city limits, grew on Long Island and northern New Jersey during the 1950s and 1960s, peaking at about 1969. Since then, the manufacturing job loss has been gentler in the suburbs (45 percent) than in the five boroughs (70 percent). Average wages, meanwhile, are actually lower in the city.[5] Rather, high land costs, indifferent policies, and numerous rezonings ended up pushing aside blue-collar workspace in favor of office, residential, and retail.

Now, at the dawn of the twenty-first century, real estate pressures, already fierce because of high land prices, stand to get worse because of zoning decisions that are encroaching upon the city's remaining manufacturing land. These policies are threatening exactly the type of industrial company—small, specialized, with a client base nearby—that seems to have found a natural home in New York City. Rather than leftovers from previous generations, these are manufacturers made for the postindustrial age. Three-quarters of New York City's industrial businesses have been created in the last twenty-five years. Eighty percent have fewer than twenty employees. Together they contribute $1.7 billion in taxes to the city treasury.[6] They all need space to survive and expand.

For a picture of the vitality of the manufacturing sector today, visit the Greenpoint Manufacturing and Design Center (GMDC), a nonprofit that started out in the early 1990s with one former jute mill in northern Brooklyn, where manufacturing companies could lease space and which has since, because of demand, expanded to four buildings. The center has a vacancy rate of about zero percent, and a waiting list of thirty companies.[7] The reason tenants come here, aside from below-market rents and a well-managed plant, is that they know their landlord will not convert to condos when the neighborhood becomes hot. The complex houses about seventy small businesses: food processors, jewelers, cabinet makers, and a company that pleats fabrics for the fashion industry. L. Bruno Holst, a woodworker who runs a three-man shop there, moved out of two other spaces in the past decade—one was turned into condos, the other offices—before getting into the GMDC. "Not every kid can grow up and become a computer programmer," he said. "Some people like to work with their hands."[8]

Cities are defined by the diversity of activities that transpire within them, and New York does more than most: it sleeps, shops, goes to movies, stages musicals, pushes papers, and, once in a while, New York even makes things. The paradox of New York's economic resurgence since the 1975 fiscal crisis is that as more people want to live here, more employers want to move to the suburbs. When large investment banks balk, elected officials give them prompt attention and generous incentives. Small companies like Royal Wine have to work harder to get noticed. And yet production workers get paid better than restaurant and retailer employees.[9] Industrial companies diversify the economic base for times when our financial/investment/real estate sector hits bottom. They serve as an essential link in supply chains to other businesses around the city and provide jobs for immigrants and minorities.[10] But perhaps the best reason New York has for holding on to its industrial jobs is that they are already here.

How SoHo Got Chic

Before CBS and Time Warner, before Merrill Lynch and Morgan Stanley, before HIP and AIG, New York City was once the nation's capital of industry. In 1910, industrial sector jobs, including manufacturing, transportation, utilities, and warehousing, accounted for more than half of all employment in the city. Joshua B. Freeman notes that after World War II, New York had more manufacturing jobs than Philadelphia, Detroit, Los Angeles, and Boston combined.[11] (Now, there are more manufacturing jobs within the city of L.A. than in New York.[12]) At some point in the twentieth century, Domino refined sugar here, E. R. Squibb produced pharmaceutical drugs, Emerson made radios and televisions, and Benson & Hedges rolled cigarettes. But the character of industrial New York was defined by small, specialized firms that did subcontracting work for larger companies. A typical New York manufacturer employed twenty-five workers, compared to fifty-nine nationally. This model made real estate a defining element of industrial Manhattan. Workers pulled racks of clothing along the side streets of the Garment District from one stage of production to the next as if the city were just one giant open-air factory. Printing companies were located in one of three neighborhoods depending on whether their customers were lawyers (Downtown), advertising firms (Madison Avenue), or catalogers (the General Post Office). The city's industrial economy was therefore particularly vulnerable as bulk production forced aside small-batch work and large manufacturers vertically integrated their assembly in places where land was cheaper.[13]

The small-batch production model dictated New York's industrial architecture also. The cast-iron lofts of SoHo—at the time called "The Valley"—were not built to suit one large corporate client. Instead, they were designed for maximum flexibility, with wide floors and high ceilings, appropriate for a sewing shop, machinery, storage, offices, or showrooms—as well as for the artists' studios, galleries, and clothing boutiques that moved in later. The conversion of Lower Manhattan into first live/work and, eventually, a living and spending neighborhood began innocently—the creative class was merely picking up the slack left by departing industrial companies. But even then, just because some manufacturers vacated did not mean that all the old companies were dying. Sharon Zukin's 1978 study of thirty-four loft buildings found that 81 percent of businesses that had moved had done so because the landlord wanted to go residential.[14] The first loft laws in the 1970s permitted only artists to live in manufacturing zones, but eventually the definition of "artist" grew to encompass those who might just dabble in art on the side and then became entirely irrelevant, which is why SoHo lofts can go for $2 million today.[15]

And so it happened, not just in SoHo, but in Washington Market (rechristened TriBeCa), Chelsea, Fulton Landing (a.k.a. DUMBO), and now Williamsburg. Bohemia moved from the crowded East Village garret to the unbroken vista of a warehouse floor. As the Manhattan loft world became the domain of the upper class, bohemia moved to the outer boroughs. Cool has, for some time, been defined to be the neighborhood that is just about to "turn"—from a semi-industrial, semipoor, or semiminority neighborhood to a white, upper-middle-class residential one. "As you travel further out on the L train," a Brooklyn real estate brokerage says in its promotional material, "the area becomes less gentrified (and more affordable), but like every other 'happening' New York neighborhood, it won't last."[16] Repurposing is in; shabby is chic. The trendiest neighborhood for restaurants is the former Meatpacking District. New York's glamour class—Diane von Furstenberg, Edward Norton, Cindy Sherman—has adopted as its pet charity the High Line, an abandoned elevated freight railroad that is being turned into a meticulously sculpted park.[17]

The way a neighborhood turns, at least the way an industrial neighborhood turns, is that people break the law. They move into buildings that are zoned for industry and sleep on warehouse floors and install their own plumbing. The city Department of Buildings rarely enforces land-use rules, however, so it doesn't *feel* like breaking the law. When inspectors try to crack down, they get no respect. After a December 2000 eviction of sixty people from a warehouse in DUMBO, city councilors complained about needless homelessness, and Mayor Giuliani quickly imposed a moratorium on further evictions. It turned out that 120 other buildings were under investigation for fire safety violations at the time, and an official estimated that illegal conversions involved "probably a thousand buildings—I'm talking just Brooklyn—and 10,000 tenants."[18] In a city with a chronic housing shortage, it is hard to care about illegal conversions, and it is even harder to care if you are an elected official. After all, people vote; factories don't.

Landlords who actually want to convert legally may apply to a mayorally appointed board called the Board of Standards and Appeals (BSA), arguing that they cannot make any money unless they go residential. This form of spot zoning does not get much press scrutiny, but over time it makes a difference. The BSA granted eighty residential variances in industrially zoned areas of Williamsburg and Greenpoint between 1995 and 2002, according to a count by the community board.[19] After a few years of illegal conversions and BSA gerrymandering, the manufacturers that remain in these areas start fielding complaints from the neighbors—idling trucks, bad smells, noise late at night—and parking tickets suddenly increase. City planning commissioners then jump in with a broad rezoning, arguing that they are merely codifying what is already taking place on the ground.

In Manhattan, commercial conversion presents as much of a problem as residential conversion—or even more so, since offices can move into most manufacturing zones "as of right." The Starrett-Lehigh building, a legendary nineteen-story monolith covering an entire city block along the Hudson River, was once a distribution center for several small companies. Built in 1932, it was designed such that trucks pulled into its bays and were raised and lowered in a central elevator to make or pick up deliveries at each floor. Architectural historian Francis Morrone writes, "Perhaps no single structure in the city says as much about the onetime industrial preeminence of New York, or about the broad-based commitment that once existed to the needs of small manufacturers."[20] After a group of investors bought it in 1998, Starrett-Lehigh became a chic address for media companies. Martha Stewart Living Omnimedia, Inside.com, SmartMoney.com, and several Web-content producers made their homes there even though it was so isolated that one company brought in its own chef to cook lunch.[21] The printing companies that had been there beforehand, meanwhile, had to move.

Rezoning for White-collar Jobs and Upscale Housing

How do you make way for a post-industrial economy? This question is a difficult one. If one waits too long, time and tax revenue are lost. Move too quickly, or in the wrong direction, and one is liable to push out industry unnecessarily. Because commercial and residential space is worth much more, rezoning a neighborhood is tantamount to doubling or tripling the monthly rent. Industrial companies that own their space—and about 40 percent do—face another dilemma.[22] Their property may be more valuable than their business, and they will be tempted to sell the building, dissolve their company, and retire to Florida. Rezoning requires delicacy, but the city has often moved rashly. In the early years, perhaps that was explained by a jubilant pro-office ideology that, spurred by interested parties, bordered on the absurd. "Our destiny is in the service field," the real estate developer William Zeckendorf once said, adding that the retreat by industry was a "magnificent thing."[23]

To its credit, the white-collar economy—particularly the health and service fields—has so successfully compensated for the decline of the industrial sector that New York now has about 3.7 million jobs, the same number that it had in the early 1950s.[24] But it is another question whether industry had to decline as much as it did. For one thing, if New York was intent on maintaining its dominance in maritime trade, it would have, in the late 1940s, welcomed an offer by the Port Authority of New York and New Jersey to take control of deteriorating city-owned piers. Instead, spurned by the city, the Port Authority steered hundreds of millions of dollars worth of improvements to Port Elizabeth and Port Newark in New Jersey, which now dwarf New York City in terms of shipping volume.[25] If New York had wanted to become a modern distribution center instead of a tangle of congested highways, it would have created the railroad connections that it was sorely lacking.

But then there is a whole other category of deindustrialization that stemmed not from indifference but from hostility. Between 1945 and 1955, a series of redevelopment projects on either side of the East River—including slum clearance for Stuyvesant Town and the leveling of the slaughterhouses to make way for the United Nations—displaced 18,000 industrial jobs. One of the projects—a new civic, business, and residential center in Brooklyn—would not be fully consummated for another thirty or forty years until the construction of the MetroTech office complex.[26] Yet, after the plans were announced, one company on the site, American Safety Razor, was offered generous incentives to move to Virginia, and so it did. Mayor Wagner's reaction was to propose an industrial park on the far outskirts of Brooklyn, but he never built it.[27]

By the late 1980s and early 1990s, the city reasoned that if industrial employment had dropped by more than half, then the areas zoned for manufacturing could lose some of their fat. But looks can be deceiving. Laura Wolf-Powers has shown that much of the space in manufacturing zones is taken up by waste-transfer stations, power plants, train yards, and La Guardia and John F. Kennedy airports—all land-intensive uses serving functions that are essential to the city's economy.[28] Just 7 percent of the entire city's building area is used by manufacturing.[29] One could equally argue—based on provisions made by the 1961 zoning amendment—that New York has space for 3 million residents who don't exist.[30] But accommodating that population would require dense resettlement of the distant corners of Queens and Brooklyn that are beyond the reach of subways. The problem is not how many jobs or homes can exist, but rather where. People want to live in the same areas where today's small industrial users settled ten or fifteen years ago, places that are close to the center of the city and near transportation. That is why the inner ring of industrial districts outside Manhattan has become a battleground in the fight between jobs and housing and the focus of rezoning efforts under the Bloomberg administration.

One such area is Greenpoint and Williamsburg, two contiguous Brooklyn neighborhoods across the East River from Manhattan that were rezoned in May 2005. The waterfront was turned into a residential area, with significant public access to the shore, and that was considered a rational use of space even by boosters of industry. More controversial was the rezoning in the heart of the neighborhoods, where forty-five mixed-use blocks were given an MX designation.[31] MX indicates that either residential or light manufacturing can locate there, and city planners claimed the zone would actually preserve industry insofar as it is not forcing existing businesses to move or preventing new manufacturers from locating there. But practically speaking, MX means that whoever is willing to pay more for the land will eventually win out. Housing developers will actually receive property-tax abatements for erecting multifamily buildings there, luxury or not, as they do for apartments erected almost anywhere outside Manhattan.[32] Furthermore, MX replaces a "special purpose" district designation in North Williamsburg that basically required any lot currently used for manufacturing to stay manufacturing even after a change in owners and permitted any lot used for housing to continue to be used for housing. "Virtually every planning professional and developer who we have spoken with agrees that MX will do nothing to preserve the industrial jobs," Adam Friedman, executive director of the New York Industrial Retention Network, said. Some ninety companies, employing 4,000 people, are at risk.[33]

Two other Brooklyn neighborhoods farther south, Red Hook and Gowanus, are expected to be next in line. Low-lying apartment buildings, high weeds, public housing projects, and factories dot the landscape. Parts of the two neighborhoods have been designated as an Empire Zone—a state program that provides tax credits—and companies participating in the program invested $35.2 million and created 450 new jobs in just one year, 2004.[34]

Yet, industrial companies are not able to create many more. John's Gourmet Salads, a one-hundred-employee company that prepares salads for gourmet delis in Manhattan, moved its operations to Pennsylvania and Delaware in mid-2005, after unsuccessfully trying to expand in Red Hook.[35] Amtronics, an electronic parts manufacturer, ended up selling out to an out-of-state competitor after the city denied its request for more parking. Trucks at the Snapple Beverage Company distribution center began getting tickets in 2000 for what they had been doing for years: waiting in line while letting their engines idle.[36] "It becomes more and more difficult to work in an environment where you have baby carriages," said Brian Coleman, CEO of the GMDC. "The cop writing a ticket for one of your trucks is just doing his job. He doesn't know that the person who called to complain is upstairs in an illegal conversion."[37]

Meanwhile, the Port Authority has agreed to give six piers it operates in Red Hook to the city to create a cruise-ship terminal. That will bring in 330 jobs—but no one has suggested a way to preserve the 600 to 750 jobs provided by a cargo company that began operating there ten years ago, and which has seen its annual shipping volume increase from 18,211 containers to 130,000.[38] Kate Ascher, a city economic development official, invited community residents at a recent meeting to come up with ways to more appropriately landscape the surrounding area given the change in use. "I think that's something we need to solve, not just work on, before the fancy people from the Queen Mary show up," she said.[39] Ah, the decline of industry is a magnificent thing, indeed.

Applying the Brakes

Former Housing Commissioner Starr mused in the 1980s that manufacturers had more important things to worry about, like competition from abroad, than being priced out of their neighborhoods.[40] To the extent that that was ever entirely true, it is much less so today. The city commissioned a survey in 2004 of 469 industrial businesses and asked them to rank, by importance, fourteen possible challenges to doing business in New York City. Real estate costs ranked third, parking tickets eighth, foreign competition came in twelfth. (Business insurance and health insurance came in first and second, respectively.) The same survey found that more than 50 percent of industrial companies plan to expand—fewer than half of those can do so where they are currently located.[41] Among printers—once a bulwark of industrial Manhattan—an independent survey in 2002 found that 31 percent planned to relocate within the following two years, a fifth of whom said they would relocate outside of New York City. The industry alone lost 12,754 jobs in Manhattan between 1980 and 2000, during which time two of its major neighborhoods were rezoned.[42]

Given all of this history, what is surprising is not so much the brashness of policymakers, but rather how conscious they were of the damage that land use changes would cause. The steps that officials took to retain industry were limited, half-hearted, or lacking in any sort of follow-through. In 1974, the city council prohibited large retail stores of more than 10,000 square feet from opening in manufacturing zones in order to prevent land values from rising.[43] (Retail stores, like offices, are usually permitted in manufacturing zones.) But the law didn't apply to stores like Home Depot or Staples. In 1988, a report by the city's Public Development Corporation, the precursor to the Economic Development Corporation, outlined rezoning in Long Island City, Queens, and recommended including a protected manufacturing area—but it was never created.[44] Current tax credit packages that are frequently used to prevent financial companies from moving to New Jersey are often inaccessible to industrial companies. The Relocation and Employment Assistance Program requires improvements worth a minimum of $25 a square foot, which is beyond the reach of many small companies, and the Industrial Commercial Incentive Program is geared toward property owners, whereas manufacturers tend to be renters.[45]

Mayor Bloomberg, while aggressively rezoning inner-ring neighborhoods, has earned plaudits from some corners for understanding the value of the industry he is displacing. His administration promised in January 2005 to establish seventeen areas throughout the city as Industrial Business Zones (IBZ), a new designation that creates an extra level of protection for the companies inside the boundaries.[46] But the IBZ's will not prohibit offices or retail, the way that similar districts do in Chicago.[47] Furthermore, a little comparative analysis shows where Bloomberg's priorities lie: industrial companies that choose to relocate in IBZ's qualify for $1,000 per employee for moving expenses. Shortly afterward, the administration agreed to lure businesses from outside New York to Lower Manhattan by promising tax credits worth $3,000 per employee, *per year for the next twelve years.*[48] Besides, Bloomberg has put off his most important industrial retention initiatives. His administration set aside $4 million to help industrial companies displaced by MX zoning in Williamsburg, but the program's details had still not been worked out six months later, after businesses had already begun to get eviction notices.[49]

Looking back, the best thing the city ever did for manufacturing was the 1961 zoning amendment, a massive undertaking that was the first and so far the only system-wide revision of the original 1916 zoning plan. The authors of the 1961 amendment hardly cared about the future of industry and, in fact, reduced the acreage in which manufacturing could be located. But they also replaced a hierarchical scheme—whereby housing could be located anywhere, offices could be located anywhere but the residential zones, and manufacturing could only be located in manufacturing zones—with a segregated system, whereby each use had to stay, more or less, within its own zone. Over time, as manufacturing land got cheaper and residential land got more expensive, these segregated zones kept apartment buildings out of the hair of manufacturers.

In other words, zoning became a means to subsidize manufacturing, but it is a subsidy that the city has, time and time again, whittled away. Now, as the city attempts to address not just its housing shortage but specifically its affordable-housing shortage, it will likely continue to do so. It will be up to planners to carefully draw those boundaries to preserve the industrial companies that now exist. It will be up to the mayor and other politicians to fulfill promises they have made to those businesses that will be displaced. The conflict between jobs and housing is real, and not pretty, but in the end, it is not a conflict at all. The advocates pushing for low-income apartments and the advocates pushing for industrial jobs are looking out for the same people: working-class immigrants and minorities without much education. What is the point of providing them with shelter if, at the same time, the city is destroying their livelihoods? Assemblyman Lopez said that affordable housing is more important than retaining jobs. Perhaps, but without jobs, people will not be able to afford much housing.

Notes

1. Julian E. Barnes, "A Venerable Kosher Winery Is Heading for New Jersey," *New York Times*, January 2, 2000, sec. 14, 8, accessed via LexisNexis online database, www.nexis.com; Eitan Segal, director of public relations for the Royal Wine Corp., interview by author, November 21, 2005.

2. Carol Abrams, assistant commissioner for communications for the New York City Department of Housing Preservation and Development, e-mail message to author, December 6, 2005. See also, New York City Department of Housing Preservation and Development, "Mayor Bloomberg Announces First Affordable Housing Development in Greenpoint-Williamsburg Waterfront Area," press release, October 7, 2005, http://www.nyc.gov/html/hpd/html/for-researchers/pr-10-07-05.html (accessed December 13, 2005).

3. Michael Calderone, "The Hip Get Square as New Condos Turn Williamsburg into Battery Park City," *New York Observer*, September 26, 2005, 13.

4. City of New York, "New York Industrial Policy: Protecting and Growing New York City's Industrial Job Base," January 2005, 7, http://www.nyc.gov/html/sbs/pdf/articles/white-paper.pdf# (accessed 13 December 2005).

5. Bureau of Labor Statistics, U.S. Department of Labor, "State and Area Employment, Hours and Earnings." Area: New York: New York City (1950–2002), Nassau-Suffolk (1952–2002); New Jersey: Newark (1960–2002), Statewide (1947–2002), adjusted to omit employment in southern New Jersey region by subtracting Vineland-Millville-Bridgeton (1970–2001). Industry: Manufacturing. Detail: A 1-digit Industry. Data Type: All Employees, Average Hourly Earnings.

6. City of New York, "New York Industrial Policy," 7.

7. Brian Coleman, CEO of the Greenpoint Manufacturing and Design Center, interview by author, October 19, 2005.

8. L. Bruno Holst, owner of Bear Woodworking, interview by author, October 19, 2005.

9. Zoning for Jobs Coalition, "A Critical Analysis of 'Up from the Ruins,'" memo, June 23, 2005, 2, http://www.nyirn.org/ZFJ%20Critical%20Analysis%20of%20Up%20From%20Ruins.pdf (accessed December 13, 2005). The comparison is based on New York State Department of Labor data. Self-reported wages to the Census Bureau, controlled for education level, show no discernible difference in pay between industrial and service workers. See also, Laura Wolf-Powers, "Upzoning New York City's Mixed-Use Neighborhoods: Property-Led Economic Development and the Anatomy of a Planning Dilemma," *Journal of Planning Education and Research* 24 (Summer 2005), n. 16.

10. City of New York, "New York Industrial Policy," 10.

11. Joshua B. Freeman, *Working-class New York* (New York: The New Press, 2000), 7–8.

12. Matthew Drennan, "Economy: After 1776," in *The Encyclopedia of New York City*, ed. Kenneth T. Jackson, 363 (New Haven: Yale University Press, 1995).

13. Freeman, *Working-class New York*, 10–14.

14. Sharon Zukin, *Loft Living* (Baltimore: The Johns Hopkins University Press, 1982), 34–35.

15. Nadine Brozan, "In a Changed SoHo, Legal Pentimento," *New York Times*, June 8, 2003, sec. 11, 1, accessed via LexisNexis.

16. Prudential Douglas Elliman Real Estate, "Neighborhoods: Brooklyn: Williamsburg," http://www.elliman.com/mainsite/neighborhoods/display.aspx?neighborhood=Brooklyn&listingid=0 (accessed December 13, 2005).

17. See supporters list of the Friends of the High Line at http://www.thehighline.org/community/supporters.html (accessed December 14, 2005).

18. Bruce Lambert, "Evictions Illuminate Issue of Illegal Loft Apartments," *New York Times*, December 27, 2000, sec. B, 3, accessed via LexisNexis.

19. Cited in Wolf-Powers, "Upzoning New York City's Mixed-Use Neighborhoods," 385.

20. Francis Morrone, *The Architectural Guidebook to New York City* (Salt Lake City: Gibbs-Smith, Publisher, 1994), 102–3.

21. Christopher Gray, "Streetscapes/Starrett-Lehigh Building; Time of Change for a Modern Industrial Landmark," *New York Times*, May 11, 1998, sec. 11, 5, accessed via LexisNexis.

22. City of New York, "New York Industrial Policy," 7.

23. Quoted in Freeman, *Working-class New York*, 168.

24. Bureau of Labor Statistics, U.S Department of Labor, "State and Area Employment, Hours and Earnings." Area: New York: New York City (1950–2002). Industry: Total Non-Farm. Detail: Total Nonagricultural. Data Type: All Employees.

25. Freeman, *Working-class New York*, 161–65.

26. Robert Fitch, *The Assassination of New York City* (London: Verso, 1993), 46.

27. Freeman, *Working-class New York*, 147–50.

28. Laura Wolf-Powers, "Why Job-Killing Rezonings Don't Make Sense: A Response to the Manhattan Institute," Pratt Institute Center for Community Development, June 2005, http://www.prattcenter.net/pol-response.php (accessed December 13, 2005).

29. Pratt Institute Center for Community Development, "Making It in New York: The Manufacturing Land Use and Zoning Initiative" Municipal Arts Society, 2001, chapter 4, 1, http://www.prattcenter.net/pol-mluzi.php (accessed December 13, 2005).

30. Michael Kwartler, "Zoning," in *The Encyclopedia of New York City*, ed. Kenneth T. Jackson, 363 (New Haven: Yale University Press, 1995), 288.

31. New York City Department of City Planning, "Greenpoint-Williamsburg Rezoning: Adopted Rezoning," map, May 2005, http://www.nyc.gov/html/dcp/pdf/greenpointwill/adopted_zoning_map_changes.pdf (accessed December 13, 2005).

32. Brad Lander and Laura Wolf-Powers, "Remaking New York City: Can Prosperity Be Shared and Sustainable?" Pratt Institute, November 2004, 10, http://www.prattcenter.net/pubs/remakingnyc.pdf.

33. Adam Friedman, testimony to the City Council of New York, City Council Hearing on the Rezoning of the Greenpoint/Williamsburg Waterfront, April 4, 2005.

34. Zoning for Jobs Coalition, "A Critical Analysis of 'Up from the Ruins,'" 4.

35. Jeffrey Levi, CEO of John's Gourmet Salads, interview by author, December 8, 2005.

36. Jonathan Bowles, "Red Hook and Gowanus Reborn," *Center for an Urban Future*, August 5, 2002, http://www.nycfuture.org/content/reports/report_view.cfm?repkey=83 (accessed November 3, 2005).

37. Coleman, interview by author, October 19, 2005.

38. For number of new jobs, see Port Authority of New Jersey and New York, "Port Authority

Begins Process to Transfer Control of Brooklyn's Piers to New York City," press release, December 8, 2005. For existing jobs and cargo volume, see Charles V. Bagli, "Is a Blue-Collar Future a Luxury on the Waterfront?" *New York Times*, February 4, 2004, sec. B, 1, accessed via LexisNexis. See also Hugh Son, "Shipping Company Gets the Hook, Not the Hook," *New York Daily News*, August 12, 2004, http://www.nydailynews.com (accessed December 7, 2005).

39. Matthew Grace, "Pier Watch," *Real Estate*, November 29, 2005, http://www.observer.com/the-realestate/2005/11/pier-watch.html (accessed December 13, 2005).

40. Roger Starr, *The Rise and Fall of New York City* (New York: Basic Books, 1985), 75.

41. City of New York, "New York Industrial Policy," 13–14.

42. "Printed in New York: The Transformation of New York City's Printing Industry," *New York Industrial Retention Network*, October 2002, 41, http://www.nyirn.org/Printed%20In%20NY%20Full%20document%20w%20Cvr&TOC.pdf (accessed December 13, 2005).

43. Department of City Planning, "New Opportunities for a Changing Economy" (City of New York, 1993), 76.

44. Zoning for Jobs Coalition, "A Critical Analysis of 'Up from the Ruins,'" 5.

45. City of New York, "New York Industrial Policy," 14, 32.

46. Ibid., 15–17.

47. Pratt Institute Center, "Making it in New York," Appendix B, 2.

48. New York City Economic Development Corporation, "Commercial Expansion Program," http://www.newyorkbiz.com/Business_Incentives/Tax_Benefits/Tax_Benefits_c.html (accessed December 7, 2005).

49. Paul Moses, "Eve of Construction," *Village Voice*, December 2, 2005, http://www.villagevoice.com/news/0549,moses,70653,5.html (accessed December 8, 2005).

GUYS, DOLLS, AND DEALS
Old and New Times Square

Marshall Berman

It doesn't matter what you wear
Just as long as you are there.
—"Dancing in the Streets," Martha and the Vandellas

My recent book on Times Square, *On the Town: One Hundred Years of Spectacle in Times Square* (2006), is a celebration of what the architect Rem Koolhaas, in his wonderful book *Delirious New York: A Retroactive Manifesto for Manhattan* (1978), calls "Manhattanism, or the culture of congestion." In addition to the square's blatant congestion of people, and of buildings, and of cars, and of signs, I highlight the square's congestion of *meaning*. I portray it as a place where we can drown, or fight to stay afloat, in a superabundance of meanings.

My book goes back to when the square was New York's Uptown, known as the "Longacre." I start with the Metropolitan Opera House at the square's south end in the 1880s, built just after the invention of the light bulb and constructed to produce electrically driven spectacles. The new electric spectacles became a tremendous success, and provided a model for the city's theater industry, which moved uptown en masse in the 1880s and 1890s and built a new generation of theaters that depended as much on electric power as on any star. New York's sex industry followed the opera uptown and embedded itself in the capacious new brownstones on east-west side streets. The subway had not yet arrived, but there was an abundance of trolley lines with their glittering silver tracks. Within a decade after Edison's invention, this place became New York's prime entertainment center, featuring state-of-the-art electrified theaters, giant electric signs—"fire signs," they called them—and shining new restaurants and cabarets featuring

While the cleaned-up Times Square is now a safe place for couples and families, many of the oversized vinyl billboards have none of the pizzazz of the inventive electric signs of former years. The vapid people pictured in the giant advertisements tower above the vibrant crowds of ordinary folks below.

great expanses of glass and walls of mirrors where people could see themselves and each other more vividly than ever. Great crowds of people were drawn here right away. This is where Theodore Dreiser's Sister Carrie came to rise and shine, and where her ex-lover Edward Hurstwood came to unravel and crash.

At the start of the twentieth century, the Times came. Its skyscraper headquarters brought a new name and created a new scale in the air. It equated the square with America's new and expanding mass media and with a new scale of corporatization. That same winter, 1905, another new mass medium opened up: the subways. The Interborough Rapid Transit (IRT) and Brooklyn-Manhattan Transit (BMT) terminated at Times Square. They linked it with the Bronx, with Queens, with Coney Island, and with the farthest-flung immigrant neighborhoods in the newly consolidated "greater New York." These subways, open all night, created a new scale underground and mobilized the biggest and densest crowds that not only New York but perhaps any city had ever seen.

Shortly before World War I, the theater industry did its first audience surveys. It found that a very large chunk of its audience were office workers under forty, from the big new buildings going up around the square and from the garment center just to the south. *Office* workers—not many sewing machine operators were in those first crowds (they came in the 1920s when movie palaces opened up) but plenty who worked telephones, switchboards, typewriters, teletypes. These young workers, often immigrants from Europe or from small-town America, worked long hours but apparently had energy to burn. After work they stayed Downtown and watched and ate and drank and danced, and often didn't go home till after midnight. New York's subway system ran all night and made a mass night life possible. Before I was born, my parents lived that life fairly intensely. On the D train heading back to the Bronx, they acted out the plays they had just seen the way *they* would have played them.

As I gathered material on Times Square and did the early studies that led to my book, I noticed how much I was writing about *women*. This was partly because of who I am, a man who loves women and who will write about them any chance I get. But it was also because of what the square was: a place that brought enormous numbers of women together. In the great crowds that poured out of the subway, down from the elevated trains, and off the trolleys, there was an amazing variety of classes and ethnicities: cooks and bakers, waitresses and seamstresses, millinery workers and saleswomen (in a posthat society, it is hard to convey the importance of hats in New York's political economy and culture until the 1960s), maids, office cleaners, typists, stenographers, salesgirls for a wide range of commodities, actresses and singers and dancers, and teachers and choreographers and coaches—in all the forms of dance, from ballet to burlesque, from dancehall hostesses to the Ziegfeld Follies and later the Rockettes—wardrobe mistresses and costumers and dressers, telephone operators, fashion models, theater and cinema ushers (one immortalized by Hopper), nightclub hatcheck girls, office clerks, bookkeepers, and on and on. My mother, Betty Berman, spent most of her seventy-year work life around the square, at first by accident, later by design: Times Square was where "smart women" went, she said. Aline Bernstein, a famous theatrical designer of my parents' generation, was born and grew up in one of the actors' boardinghouses that lined Broadway before twentieth-century skyscrapers pushed them out. She used a lovely phrase to describe the crowds of young actresses in the summer, dressed in their gaudiest colors, going round to agents and booking offices in search of work in the fall: "They embroidered Broadway with themselves." Was there ever a public space where such a wide range of women could feel at home? where women could feel that they were putting their mark on the street just by being there?

There is a rare silent movie that can offer us a clue to Times Square's peculiar appeal. The movie is called *Classified*; it was released in 1926. (It doesn't seem to exist in video.) Its heroine is Babs Comet, a switchboard operator in a daily newspaper's classified ad department just off the square. A title captures her in a great one-liner: "Her earning capacity fell short of her yearning capacity." Babs lives Uptown, and she gets to work in a way that the titles tell us many girls do: she stands on Broadway and hitches rides with guys driving downtown. There is a striking scene with Babs and one of these guys in a convertible: He gropes her more intensely as they get farther downtown. But she has perfect timing, she knows just how far she can go, and as the driver stops for a light (I think at Forty-seventh Street), she leaps out of the car with a ballerina's finesse, lands on a traffic island, waves goodbye to the cursing man, and arrives at work tousled but exhilarated and intact. Apparently the girls at the switchboard all do this, and they trade escape stories. *Classified* presents itself as a light comedy, but it is hard not to find this behavior startling. Can't these girls imagine what could happen? You can see why the place in New York where the most people were likely to go was also the subject of the most sermons and admonitions telling people *not* to go. But it wasn't only the churchy and the old fashioned who ran it down. Secular modernists like Walter Lippmann, Lewis Mumford, and Jane Addams denounced this place as vehemently as any divine. It was a secular reformer who anointed Times Square as "the capital of dangerous love." Appalling, but also alluring, to all who yearn for "dangerous love" and imagine it as a thrill. Interesting to think that so many of the most passionate yearners have been working girls.

One of the signatures of Times Square's spectacle, from then to now, has been its concentration of electrically powered fire signs. Many of the best have been signs of women. A late-1880s photo of the Casino Theater, across from the Met, shows a spread of life-size models of women mounted on its facade. Dreiser liked to hang out with the Casino's chorus girls; this is where he places his *Sister Carrie* and portrays her rising from its chorus meteorically to be a star. At the book's end, Hurstwood has crumpled into a drunken bum in rags. He lives in a flophouse on the Bowery—it will let him in at night, but meanwhile he is forced to tramp uptown and downtown. At Times Square, he can't resist the light: "'I'll just go down Broadway,' he said to himself. When he reached Forty-second Street, the fire signs were already burning bright."

As he passes the Casino, he sees Carrie's sign on the street. He starts shouting at the model: "You've got it, you better give me some." Then he realizes, with horror and self-disgust, what he has just done. "I'll quit this," he says. Within a couple of pages he kills himself, and the book ends. What Hurstwood does in Times Square is to confuse a sign with a living woman. In fact, this confusion will turn out to be one of the square's life signs.

In 1909, a sensational fifty-foot fire sign, celebrating Heatherbloom Petticoats, Silk's Only Rival, stopped traffic at the Square's north end. It had an elaborate electronic program that flashed the impact of a blizzard on a woman's body. She was wearing a typical pre–World War I long skirt, maybe with many layers. Sheets of wind and rain swept up her body and undressed her, leaving her in a Heatherbloom that clung to her body and showed, in profile, what a youthful woman looked like—she would be stripped to her profile, and then a minute later be out in the storm again. (She opened the floodgate for Marilyn Monroe forty years later, at nearly the same location, in *The Seven Year Itch*, undressed by underground streams of steam from the subway.) A couple of years later, Pierre Loti, French writer of soft-core romances, in a piece for the *Century Magazine* on his "Impressions of New York," writes lyrically about Times Square:

> The electricity flows in rivers [and] disports itself as a great spectacle....I
> ascend to the top of the Times Building, one of the boldest of skyscrapers....
> The most diabolical sign of all is the face of a woman, which occupies as much
> space in the sky as the Great Bear. During the few seconds she shines, her left
> eye winks as though in enticing appeal.

Loti is enthralled by this electronic woman's mystery. But he thinks he knows the key. "What on earth can they be selling down there?" The square's aura of mystery has always been a *commercial* mystery.

Some of the most luminous visions of women in Times Square were created by the movies in the 1930s. Here I will mention only three: Ruby Keeler in *42nd Street* (1933); Wini Shaw singing "Lullaby of Broadway," leading a dancing crowd up to a skyscraper roof in *Gold Diggers* (1935); and, all through the 1930s, the animated adventures of Betty Boop. The first two visions were created and choreographed by Busby Berkeley, the third by Max and Dave Fleischer, with the voice of Mae Questel. In all three, the heroines are poor girls from the wrong side of the tracks. In all, they engage in high-risk behavior. What would their mothers say? In Times Square, a girl has to court danger if she wants to make her mark.

In *42nd Street*, Keeler's ability to dance in the street and to animate a theatrical genre that signifies joy, even at the nadir of the Depression, is a parable of hope for America's power to come back from the collective misery that afflicts everybody; holding together an enormous and conflicting cast signifies the capacity to hold together a torn country.

"Lullaby of Broadway" is about the dream life of a chorus girl, whom we see as the night world's proletarian. She is played by Wini Shaw, a virtually unknown starlet, who shortly after *Gold Diggers* totally disappeared. She lives in crowds, yet feels lonely and terrified. Dick Powell, the star's mentor in *42nd Street* is here again to hold the heroine's hand. He not only urges her to join the crowd but assures her she has the strength to lead it. She seizes the day, and for one magic moment, the prophecy seems to work: she dances a crowd up a spiral staircase to a penthouse with a spectacular vista. But then the crowd overwhelms her and unintentionally pushes her off. Her plunge is horrific— but then we see it was all a dream. The movie's second most powerful moment is one where she looks up at us, and suddenly the lines of her face become the map of a city; a little later, just before she strikes the earth, the city becomes her face.

Betty Boop, made right here at 1600 Broadway, highlights the grittiness of street life in Times Square. Its heroine fights to emancipate herself from her outer-borough Jewish immigrant parents; in some episodes, because it is the Depression, she becomes their sole support. The bad news is, she is forced to sell her labor power—which means, above all, her energy and charm—in order to live. The good news is that, in Times Square, there really is a market for energy and charm like hers. She participates in a life that includes sex, drugs, hot jazz, high risks. Her workplace is a personality market that swallows up many of the people around her. But she always lands on her feet, and she laughs. When she sings, "They can't take away my boop-boop-a-doop," she affirms the comic spirit of New York's working girls, even in tragic times.

But even as the Depression created poetic visions of women at home in Times Square, it generated an undertow that destroyed that home. In the early 1930s, several of Forty-second Street's grandest theaters closed, including the woman-friendly Ziegfeld Follies at the New Amsterdam. Four of the largest houses morphed into burlesque houses—"went the way of all flesh," was the joke. At first, people didn't realize how much this change would skewer the street's sexual balance. But within a few years, Forty-second Street was not only virtually all male but aggressively threatening to women. For the first time in Times Square's history, "the deuce," Forty-second Street between Broadway and Eighth Avenue, became sexually segregated. A polarity developed between the closed, masculinized deuce and the expansive, inclusive "bowtie," the X-shaped intersection of Broadway and Seventh Avenue, around the corner. Mayor La Guardia, moving to the right at the end of the thirties and seeking political support from churches, conducted a long campaign against burlesque. His hope, he said, was to restore the deuce's lost grandeur. During World War II, he finally got backing from secular courts, and the burlesque houses were shut down. What took their place, however, was not grand theater—the theaters had closed in the first place because they couldn't make money on a market-driven street—but cheap cinema, mainly Westerns and gangster and combat films—*This Gun For Hire, Northwest Mounted Police, Bailout at 40000*, and hundreds of genre films like these—geared to an entirely male audience. The deuce grew even more gender-segregated than before and hostile not only to women but even to "fairies," the style of homosexuals who had filled the street in its glory days. What gay people called "rough trade" was its signature style now.

In August 1945, the day of the Japanese surrender, Times Square was the setting for the *Life* cover photo by Alfred Eisenstadt that became one of America's classic icons: a sailor and a nurse, apparently strangers but locked in a passionate embrace and surrounded by a smiling crowd. But this scene could only have taken place in one part of the square, within its Broadway bowtie. Neither the couple nor the crowd could have materialized on a post-Depression Forty-second Street. The bowtie of 1945 could still be seen to represent an open, expansive, democratic America. The deuce, a street without women, seemed to be turning slowly into one of the seedier parts of the Third World.

After the war, the square got dingier, filled up with cheap arcades and ambiguous curiosity shops, with blacks, Latins, Asians, and Central and Eastern Europeans, with tourists and refugees. It became the most deeply integrated, multinational space in New York and a wonderland for people who liked looking at people. (It still is.) For grungy high school kids like my friends and me, just learning to use the subway system, without much money to spend but good eyes and ears, it was a perfect place to hang out. When we got back home to the Bronx or Brooklyn or Washington Heights, we could read in the paper or hear a solemn Walter Winchell on the air: "When is something going to be done about Times Square?"

The musical *Guys and Dolls* (1950; endlessly revived) perfectly captured the discourse that had gathered around the square. Writers Frank Loesser and Abe Burrows, who had spent most of their lives there, could see the neighborhood was vulnerable. Plenty of its own people were sick of it. One of the most striking of these is the show's leading "doll," Sister Sarah Brown. Sarah works for the Salvation Army's Forty-second Street Mission and makes fiery speeches denouncing the deuce. "I'd like to take a pickax," she says, "and smash Broadway end to end." But even as she flares up with rage and fury, she is the most beautiful girl on the street. The leading "guy," the gambler and night-person Sky Masterson, tells her she is out of touch with her deepest needs: she belongs to the city, and she belongs to the night, and in denouncing them, she denies herself. He sings, "You have wished yourself a Scarsdale Galahad / A breakfast-eating Brooks Brothers type."

What if Times Square really *is* torn down, if the night world becomes a day world—we could say a breakfast world—if the "street" is replaced by the "straight"? Where does she think she will find somebody to love? She sings, "I'll know," but we can see she hasn't a clue. However, after much plot, Loesser and Burrows will bail her out. Broadway's buildings will stay up for awhile, but Sarah's ideological pickax will cleave the people. The show ends with a grand cleanup at the Mission, where Sky and all the square's night people are born again. Then the guy and the doll get married. Then they are driven to their honeymoon by the police. (Is it an allegory of urban renewal? Or of the Cold War? We'll never know.)

In the 1960s, it was the market that swung the ax against the square. On the bowtie, in just a few years, many of the best buildings and public spaces were destroyed: Times Tower, the Astor Hotel, Lindy's (I was one of its last customers: on Friday I enjoyed its strudel, as fine as ever, on Sunday it shut down), Tofinetti's, the Automat, the Paramount, the Roxy. I am sure there were more. It is a tribute to the resiliency of urban space that, even after these assaults, the square still felt like itself. When the Times sold the Times Tower, and it morphed into a giant mausoleum, I wondered why none of the other papers ran a headline: "Times Sells Out Times Square." Then I reflected—they all had real estate departments, all in search of the best deals. Meanwhile, on the deuce, its pornography and sex services, which for years were just segments in a large ensemble of retail activities, made such spectacular profits that they crowded out virtually everything else. The street's excellent secondhand magazine shops, which I had patronized since high school, evolved into pornographic magazine shops, then into pornographic video shops, because the profit on videotapes far surpassed the profit on what one manager called "paper goods"; then into full-service sex shops, with masturbatory film booths and live performers dancing upstairs (Disclosure: I never went upstairs). Peepland, one of the most elaborate, dominated the street with a giant eye. (I thought, left over from *The Great Gatsby*?) Customers tended to be middle-aged men with short hair and raincoats, looking a lot straighter than me. But the male crowd on the street took on a new density and nastiness.

How was it nasty? Nobody was ever nasty to me. (The worst thing that happened to me was that once, when I saw a man crack another man's skull, I couldn't get a cop.) But there was a free-floating malice toward women. If you were female, the twisted perspectives of Martin Scorsese's *Taxi Driver* were realism. The crowd treated all women not just as sex objects but as objects in a style of sex that was like rough trade. But it also seemed to hold a grudge against women for invading turf that supposedly belonged to guys alone. For nearly thirty years, until the CUNY Graduate Center moved at the end of the nineties, I taught across from Bryant Park, a block from the square. An important part of my job, not listed in the original job description, came to be walking women from my classes to the IRT Subway on Broadway and the Port Authority Bus Terminal on Eighth Avenue. I had to steer them past some aggressively creepy characters, assuring them it was no big deal but not so sure myself. We often had to go around to Fortieth or Forty-third because they found the deuce unbearable, and I couldn't sincerely say it wasn't. The other streets also had plenty of pimps, drug dealers, and (especially in the 1980s) homeless families, but women didn't seem to feel that those streets were reaching out to grab them. What made the difference? I suspect a combination of Forty-second Street's marvelous lighting, as powerful as ever in its pornographic age, and its century-old identity as a spectacle, where just to walk that block was to take an active part in the spectacle. Near the middle of the block, for years, there was an especially gross female nude with empty eyes, marked COMPLETE $10. Once, when a woman wanted to explain why we had to walk around this block and not on it, she pointed to that sign and said, "Please." I guess she was saying, "I don't want to be part of that."

Ironically, the most lurid images of women in Times Square were placed there by women who hated the square most. There was an NGO called Women Against Pornography (WAP), which became famous in the 1970s for its flying raids on pornographic bookstores and its marches demanding to TAKE BACK THE NIGHT. WAP had a recruiting table that featured an enlarged cover of *Hustler* magazine with an apparently naked woman (you could only see her legs) being thrown into a giant meat grinder. The women maintaining these tables would call, like barkers, "The murderers of women are right here. Murder is going on right here, right now. How long will we tolerate these murders? Stop the murderers NOW!" Once I asked a woman at a WAP table: "Wasn't the street bad enough without meat grinders?" She gave me a full-fledged theory of how pornography was rape—not a representation of rape, not an incitement to rape, but rape itself. (Later on I discovered the author of this theory was the legal theorist Catherine Mackinnon.) If a violent act was going on "right in front of our noses," she said, wasn't it right to scream? WAP's screams blended right in with what Times Square in those years had become.

But it wasn't just WAP's neofundamentalists who were screaming. Sometime in the 1980s, I had a graduate student who was a community organizer in the South Bronx. She was a tough woman who had dealt with plenty. Some show was running just off the square, and I said maybe her ten-year-old daughter would like it. "Are you kidding?" she said. "Bring Elena here? I'd see this street *bombed* before I'd bring her here." At that moment I knew that it *would* be bombed. In other words, I knew that the next round of municipal proposals for leveling the deuce—cleaning up the square, turning the night world into a day world, bringing in the Scarsdale Galahads—was bound to succeed. In the United States, the movement for historic preservation doesn't go back very far. But as far as it does go, educated women have always been its vanguard. (Think of Jane Jacobs and Jacqueline Kennedy Onassis, unlikely icons together.) When educated women want to bomb a neighborhood instead of fight for it, there is no way it can last.

I won't go through the long, grueling process that tore down the deuce and that brought in a gallery of world class media conglomerates—Disney/ABC, Bertelsmann, Condé Nast, Reuters, Viacom/HBO, and more—in a brand-new array of shining, tax-subsidized skyscrapers. It took a labyrinth of immensely complex billion-dollar "big deals" to get there. (Lynne Sagalyn, in her 2001 study, *Times Square Roulette: Remaking the City Icon*, threads her way through the labyrinth better than anyone.) But I want to focus on three women who played important roles in making things happen. They were part of the first generation of women to get top jobs in corporate and political management: Gretchen Dykstra, for many years the CEO of the Times Square Business Improvement District (BID); Rebecca Robertson, head of the New York State 42nd Street Development Project; and Cora Cohn of the New 42nd Street Foundation. The media called them "The Three Witches." For more than a decade, they worked together very effectively to secure court orders and to get old sites condemned and torn down and new buildings put up. At press conferences and interviews, they finished each other's sentences. But it was also striking how they dressed, how they moved, how smoothly they used their body language. They deployed WAP-like righteous rage at the square's exploitation of women, not just in the pornography of the deuce, but on the great fire signs of the bowtie selling jeans and cameras and cars. At the same time, they came on like classic Times Square babes—with a suggestion of the hip heroines of *Sex in the City*. Their patron saint was Sarah Brown, the Broadway Baby who yearned to "rip up Broadway from end to end."

(Full disclosure: I may be listed in one of Robertson's "Delete" files. In 1999 or 2000, I appeared on MSNBC with her and critic Paul Goldberger to discuss the Square's past and future. She said, "Isn't it wonderful to see Forty-second Street as a place where families can walk with their kids?" I said it was nice, but my parents had used Forty-second Street as a place to get away from their kids. I thought I saw her eyes narrow when I mentioned the red dress my mother wore when they went to the square. Later that night, I was talking about the evolution of the square's sex shops. Robertson interrupted and asked, "Have *you* been inside those shops?" I said, "Of course I have, I wouldn't talk about them if I hadn't." She exclaimed, "Why is this man allowed on television?" At first I was flattered. Does she really think I am important enough to ban from TV? Then I reflected she must talk that way to all the guys.)

So what is the square like now? Here's the paradox: it's just as bad as many old timers feared and yet a lot less bad. Remember what I was saying about *Delirious New York*, Koolhaas' marvelous "retroactive manifesto for Manhattan"? His central idea was "Manhattanism, or *the culture of congestion*." New York's creativity, he said, came from the life of *too many* in the midst of *too much*. I entirely agree; I have been trying to show New York's culture of congestion working as a congestion of *meanings*, a congestion of *ideas*. Times Square's old and new incarnations coexist and collide with each other. The crowds are bigger than ever and more diverse; there are more ethnicities, more religions, a wider spectrum of classes "blinded by the light." The Scarsdale Galahads are here in force today but so are the night people; there may even be more children of the night because the night is safer now. More people have come in, many people have been moved around, but, contrary to expectations, nobody has been pushed out. Now it is clearer than ever that there is room for everybody—this space can hold them all. Forty years ago, Motown's Martha and the Vandellas sang, "It doesn't matter what you wear / Just as long as you are there." Today's Times Square is a larger and more-vivid-than-ever incarnation of "there."

Where are the women there? It's too soon to know. But here are two vignettes. One is about the weekday crowd of teenage girls standing beneath the MTV studio on Broadway, hoping to appear on the 5 p.m. music program *TRL (Total Request Live)*. When I first saw these girls (there are some boys in this crowd, but it is overwhelmingly female), they looked silly—whistling, waving, undulating, begging to be chosen by the program's "scouts." But when I watched the program on TV, I saw that some of these high school kids from the Bronx or New Jersey were pretty smart: they knew a lot about different modes of music, and they could offer complex and sophisticated riffs. I was glad to see these active consumers of mass culture included in the production process and glad to see Times Square as a place that can link producers and consumers.

If the first item is about some of Times Square's smart girls, the second is about what my mother used to call the square's "smart women." On my last field trip through the square, in the summer of 2004, I was struck by the scene on the ground. The women on the street—costume designers, camerawomen, travel agents, dancers, tourists, students with enormous knapsacks, models with portfolios, ladies who lunched—were letting it all hang out. They were dressed in purple designer suits, clingy black dresses with slanted hems and swooping necklines, artfully slashed jeans (Were they slashed by the wearer or the producer? I could only guess.), multilayered undershirts, red combat boots (In June? Oy! I thought in my mother's voice.), five inch heels, mauve flip-flops, five hundred shades of skin and nails and hair. They looked artful, imaginative, highly individualized, terrific. Like the Parisian women in the street first described in Montesquieu's *Persian Letters* (1721), these women constituted a grand spectacle. Like the unemployed young actresses of a century ago, they embroider Broadway with themselves. On the other hand, the women on the signs above, advertising sportswear or makeup or perfume, promoting plays and CDs and films, were amazingly—what's the opposite of smart? Is it dumb or is it dead?—they looked like attempts to reinvent the giant camp pinups of the 1950s. They all seemed to have the same pink skin and blond hair and formal poses and empty smiles. Dreiser in 1900 spoke of Times Square's fire signs, but in today's signs, the fire has been put out. (These billboards suggest women's wear in Brezhnev's Red Square, and they make it clear why the Berlin Wall had to come down.) Even when a woman on a sign was naked, like the Rocawear model at Forty-seventh and Broadway, she managed to look impeccably and impermeably dressed. The flowing, curving numbers on the Morgan Stanley Building facade looked more like live women than did this latest generation of giant fire-extinguished signs.

The aura is so weird! You can feel the openness and verve in the real women on the ground, along with a massive imaginative shrinkage and devitalization in the signs of the ideal women in the air. The contrast between the ground and the air, between the square's streets and its signs, is an apt symbol of what has become of the United States in our new millennium. American feminism has had real success in enabling millions of women to direct their lives and fight to control their future on the ground. Yet, after thirty years of feminism, our collective moral life is in the hands of the old men of the Christian Right, working through the night to put women's inner light out and propel them—and all of us—back into the past.

I guess it is fitting that the Clear Channel Company of Dallas, one of the biggest American media conglomerates and one of the most prominent sponsors of the Christian Right, is said to own more billboard space than anybody in Times Square today. Is Clear Channel to blame? When accused, its people deny it: They're capitalists, and they know they can make a lot more money on hot signs than on tepid ones; that's why they came to Times Square in the first place. Blame the government—the BID, the Forty-second Street State Development Agency—they say, for censoring the air and fighting to make Times Square square. What do I think? I just don't know. But whoever is to blame, they're bound to fail. The overflowing life on the ground today proves the hopelessness of the long crusade to kill the street. Times Square is a place where, in spite of everything, modern life goes on.

GLOBAL TRANSFORMATIONS AND THE MALLING OF THE SOUTH BRONX

Susan S. Fainstein

In February 2006, the New York City Council approved the rezoning of a parcel of industrially zoned city-owned land in the South Bronx. Its purpose was to allow the Related Companies, New York's largest speculative developer, to build a million-square-foot suburban-style shopping mall on the site where the Bronx Terminal Market had operated for nearly eighty years.

The new project, to be called the Gateway Center at Bronx Terminal Market, will include a hotel, a big-box retailer, and the standard array of chain stores enclosed within a single structure. Eight existing buildings, some that have been listed on the National Register of Historic Places, will be torn down. Hundreds of well-paying jobs will be lost, and a once vital and viable business cluster will be destroyed.

The Bronx Terminal Market, a wholesale supplier to the city's ethnic restaurants and bodegas for the last eighty years, is slated to be demolished to make way for a million square-foot suburban-style enclosed shopping mall, hotel, and big-box store.

Ironically, suburban developers have largely abandoned this form of enclosed mall and instead have been constructing "town centers," designed to look like the urban downtowns now nostalgically remembered. So, while New York is busily imitating the suburbia of yesteryear, outlying municipalities, responding to their residents' desire for more meaningful urban forms, are re-creating urban-type cores.

This move to transform a piece of the South Bronx into quasisuburbia is part of a broader process that is aimed at restructuring much of New York City. It resembles transformative programs in many other American cities, where officials perceive that the industrial and wholesale market functions of earlier times are now obsolete. Real estate owners see the opportunity to increase the return on their properties by using public subsidies available for converting them to service-related uses, and investors can expect speculative gains as low-rent districts are upgraded.

The chairman of the Related Companies, which bought the market lease from the previous leaseholder, is a close friend of the city's deputy mayor for economic development. The company's plans should have been subject to political negotiation since part of their financing was coming from the city and state, the plans needed approval by locally elected public officials, and the site required rezoning for retail use. But no meaningful give and take took place. The Related Companies's glowing presentation of the project's putative benefits was never seriously challenged by any public official. Although the Bronx borough president, members of the community board, and council members expressed sympathy for the plight of the merchants, their sentiments did not move them to stand in the way of the juggernaut that was pushing the project.

The market merchants fought their displacement in court and before various city forums, including the local community board, the City Planning Commission, and the City Council. Sadly, however, the merchants lacked sufficient political influence to sway these officials either into willingness to integrate them into the Gateway project or to supply them with a suitable relocation site. By and large, officials accepted the logic that the new mall represented necessary modernization and adaptation to the service economy.

Consultants to the market merchants proposed developing an integrated wholesale and retail market similar to the successful Pike Place Market in Seattle or New York's own Chelsea Market. Construction of a combined wholesale-retail facility would have differentiated the enterprise from cookie-cutter malls around the country, exploited its urban setting, and retained existing jobs. But the developer was preselected for the site without solicitation of competitive bids or the opportunity for anyone to suggest other development strategies. Representatives of the city argued that since the developer bought the lease directly from the previous operator of the market, it was a purely private deal and thus required no competitive bidding. The city excluded affected residents and businesses from participating in planning for the area, limiting their input to reacting to the already-formulated plans. The developer provided the neighborhood with, at best, minor concessions in the form of a community benefits agreement.

From Hand Trucks to Shopping Carts

Since the 1920s, this area of the South Bronx, which lies directly beneath the Major Deegan Expressway, has been home to a quintessentially New York wholesale food market. Reflecting the city's ethnic diversity, the merchants at the Bronx Terminal Market sold their exotic produce, meats, and canned goods primarily to bodegas, African food stores, and other specialized retailers.

The market was originally located to take advantage of access to waterborne transportation on the Harlem River. It was renovated and reopened with considerable fanfare by Mayor LaGuardia in 1935, and several of the last remaining firms could trace their origins back to those early days. Subsequently the market benefited from the construction of I-95 and the Major Deegan Expressway, which provided convenient access for large trucks. During the last few decades, however, landlord neglect had resulted in decrepit structures, potholed roadways, inadequate services, grim interiors, and filthy surroundings. Those merchants who hung onto the end had suffered from the failure of the market's manager to maintain the property. Yet as late as 2005, twenty-three remaining wholesalers (down from an original peak of nearly one hundred) and their 400 employees were still generating hundreds of millions of dollars in sales.

The ability of the merchants to overcome the daunting obstacles they confronted each day came from the synergy among their firms and their advantageous location just across the Harlem River from Manhattan. By forming a cluster of similar businesses, the market firms attracted customers from the entire metropolitan area who would shop at several of the establishments in a single trip. Moreover, the merchants cooperated with each other, lending help when one was shorthanded, referring customers to adjacent businesses, and sharing information. All this, however, will end with the construction of a shopping mall on the site and the displacement of the remaining firms to scattered locations. In fact, it is doubtful that many of them can keep their customers after a move or survive without the benefits of agglomeration.

The mall intended for the South Bronx will present long, blank exterior walls, offering only a few corridors into the surrounding neighborhood. In addition, the adjacent big-box store is strongly opposed by local unions because of the employment practices of this type of merchandiser. Much of the site will be dedicated to parking decks, even though its proponents have claimed that traffic impacts will be minimal because they expect most customers to walk to the stores. The architects' renderings of the center show urbane visitors sipping cappuccino at outdoor sidewalk cafes flanking the mall. Presumably, these boulevardiers would ignore the noise, soot, exhaust, and bird droppings drifting down from the highway immediately above them.

The justification for the project primarily stems from its economic contribution rather than the physical improvements it will contribute to the area. Substantial city subsidies are involved, and taxpayers' money will be put at risk in the expectation of projected revenues and employment. The change in zoning will result in a transformation of the employment structure of the area. Where many of the market's employees (almost all of them male) had worked there for years and earned above-minimum wages, the clerks in the new retail stores will be predominantly young, low-paid women.

Urban Redevelopment and Public Policy

The Bronx Terminal Market constituted part of a larger industrial zone similar to others that defined the river banks of New York for much of the last century. A similar section of Brooklyn along the East River is being converted from manufacturing to luxury residential uses, while current plans for the west side of Midtown in Manhattan near the Hudson River involve transforming industrial space into office complexes. Formerly industrial sections of Chelsea, as in SoHo before it, have already rapidly changed into a center for arts and entertainment. The redevelopment of these latter two districts occurred largely without governmental intervention, as primarily existing structures were adapted to other, postindustrial uses. Large-scale conversion schemes encompassing new construction, however, involve public sector subsidies and land takings. Since the termination of the federal urban renewal program in 1974, these public actions have depended on local financing and public-private partnerships dominated by private-sector planning. Increasingly, they have returned to the formerly discredited pattern of dislocation that once characterized urban renewal.

In the first phase of urban renewal (from 1949 to 1964), local public authorities drew funds from the federal urban renewal program, notoriously condemned low-income neighborhoods as blighted, moved people of color from central locations, and dismissed small-scale enterprises as unworthy of preservation. Opponents of projects that would destroy small business were, like the Bronx Terminal Market merchants, excoriated for standing in the way of progress. But the resulting landscapes usually lacked architectural interest and typically failed to generate the excitement associated with urban densities. Eventually, it became evident that benefits did not usually trickle down, communities were destroyed, cleared land lay vacant for decades awaiting a developer, and "marginal" businesses, which frequently laid the groundwork for the next wave of innovation, were uprooted. Urban protest movements fought against massive redevelopment programs and succeeded in blocking numerous schemes. Some of the renewal programs triggered riots, leading to a much more cautious approach to redevelopment.

Once the dangers of wholesale demolition and new construction imitating a suburban model became fully appreciated, the federal legislation was amended to allow rehabilitation and mixed uses, to require adequate relocation of displaced residents and businesses, and to mandate citizen participation. These restrictions, however, disappeared with the end of the federal program in 1974. By now, more than thirty years later, many of the lessons of urban renewal have been forgotten as a new generation of public officials, architects, and planners has come along seeking to imprint its vision on the landscape. Consequently, while planning for New York City diverges from suburban planning in calling for much higher densities and more mixed uses, it still aims at developing an economic base that, as in the suburbs, excludes gritty industries, supports blandness, and, in the case of the Gateway Center at the Bronx Terminal Market, promotes automobile dependence and retail homogeneity. How do we explain this?

Global Forces, Economic Restructuring, and Urban Redevelopment

The most obvious explanation for current trends in redevelopment programs lies with the global restructuring of capital, which has had a number of significant consequences for cities. Beginning in the mid-1970s, a period often referred to as "post-Fordist" or "post-industrial," important changes took place in the economic structure of all the wealthy countries. Faced with declining profit rates, global competition, and the recognition that they could increase their share of gross national product without serious repercussions, owners of capital launched a major effort to bring down their costs of production and reduce the level of taxation they had to pay. Various corporate leaders followed different routes, but in aggregate their policies added up to a strategy of fighting unions, requiring givebacks from labor, lobbying for tax relief, and moving production away from high-cost locations. By threatening to move facilities to another region or out of the country altogether, they forced opponents to capitulate to their demands. The argument that stern measures were necessary in order to retain jobs provided a veil behind which their actions appeared necessary rather than voluntary.

Global competition was particularly fierce within the market for manufactured goods. Where previously Europe and the United States had occupied a virtually monopolistic position in manufacturing, now a host of Asian competitors were supplying goods of higher quality at lower costs. At the same time, developments in information technology were allowing corporations to monitor operations that were not in physical proximity to headquarters and to outsource parts of the production process.

How then did this all affect cities? It meant that capital became much more footloose. Firms could simply leave cities in search of some other place where it was cheaper to produce, so that each component of a large firm could be located in a different place. This in turn meant that cities were forced to compete to attract businesses by giving large subsidies both directly to firms and also to property developers. Another factor was the increased importance of financial and business services—and these services take place in office buildings. As older industrial cities began to see no hope of regaining their manufacturing base, they tried to capture this expanding sector of the economy by lowering its costs through providing or subsidizing space for it. And, while they were giving up on attracting manufacturers, they could endeavor to capture the retail outlets where imported goods were sold to American consumers. Retail establishments had fled inner cities in pursuit of the suburban middle class. But since cities still possessed a sizable customer base, planners and developers felt that the right retail formula could still succeed. Among the models they examined were theme parks.

The study showed the Disney Corporation to be one of the biggest influences on the contemporary appearance of cities. It is a very successful economic enterprise that has provided a template for developers by showing that shopping can be made into entertainment. If you look at a Disney park, it has some rides but mainly it consists of places to buy stuff. The structure you see may look like an old-fashioned gas station, or it may look like a haunted house, or it may look like a ranch, or it may look like a chalet in Switzerland. But whatever it looks like as fantasy, you can still go inside and buy things. Most of the goods available for purchase are not particularly useful. This model of buying nonutilitarian objects in places where buying things is fun has become part of modern retailing everywhere. The recreational aspect of shopping is achieved through the provision of amusements within the atria of malls and the creation of flashy displays and loud music within stores. Thus, the shopping mall seeks to re-create the excitement of the old downtowns through a variety of artifices that make up for their basic sameness and lack of spontaneous interaction.

The other popular shopping model, one that is totally at odds with the first, is the warehouse store. Here is where one buys the goods one has to have—towels, toilet paper, appliances, etc.—within the most mundane of settings. Unlike the five-and-dimes and hardware and dry-goods stores that once lined Main Streets and, until quite recently, New York's avenues, these giant "category killers" do not offer familiar, friendly proprietors, but they do provide off-street parking. The Gateway Center at the Bronx Terminal Market promises both these types of shopping—the enclosed mall and the big-box store.

One of the claims of the Gateway Center's developer is that the impoverished residents of the South Bronx crave the opportunity to shop at deep-discount stores. This is probably the case and is the product of the uneven economic and spatial development that has intensified in the post-Fordist period. New York has seen rising poverty and a declining median income since 1990. Competitive advantage implies nothing about the quality of life of people who live in cities. Even though growth may be a prerequisite for increased social welfare, it does not necessarily produce improvements in well-being. The economic prosperity of recent times evidently did not greatly diminish unemployment, overcome poverty, end race-and-gender-based discrimination, or integrate immigrants fully into urban society. Within New York City, even while crime rates have fallen, population has increased, and the physical appearance of the city has improved, the number of people stranded in the lowest income brackets has grown. Residents are caught in a vicious circle: they cannot afford to patronize independent shopkeepers because their wages are so low, and their wages are so low because large corporations have been able to force down the general wage rate, justifying their stinginess as required by competition.

Most of New York's recent population expansion has been the result of immigration, which has had the effect of both reinvigorating formerly desolate neighborhoods and of increasing the number of people in poverty. Like the changes in economic structure, the heightened level of immigration is a product of the transformation of the world economy. You cannot have the globalization of economic functions without also having globalization of labor, even where much of this flow of people is not legally recognized. In many parts of the city, immigrant enclaves have generated a mélange of stores purveying specialized products to satisfy the tastes of recently arrived residents. Some of these neighborhoods have even become special attractions, as fellow countrymen have sought the unique goods available within them, and residents from other parts of the city and suburbia have visited them to experience their exotic qualities. In fact, these resurrected neighborhoods now offer New York a competitive advantage over its suburban hinterland.

In view of these changes, a more imaginative city government could see an opportunity in "obsolete" facilities like the Bronx Terminal Market, which has been the principal supplier of wholesale foodstuffs to immigrant-run shops. Like the specialized manufacturing districts in Brooklyn and Queens, the Bronx market would still fill a niche in New York's contemporary economy. Whereas certain kinds of manufacturing and wholesale distribution have no need to be within the city (i.e., the production of chewing gum or bulk warehousing of dry goods), facilities that cater directly to the city's specialized service industries and small shops play an important role.

Critics of New York's economic development policies used to accuse city officials of focusing on Manhattan at the expense of the outer boroughs. Even while massive subsidies were being provided to firms threatening to leave Manhattan for New Jersey, commercial areas within Brooklyn and the Bronx were withering. The pressures of skyrocketing real estate prices in Manhattan, along with population growth, have now forced middle-class residents into parts of the city that they formerly would not have considered. The domino effect of these moves has changed the market in areas that major retailers once shunned. This has occurred at the same time that the city's Economic Development Corporation has begun to pay more attention to outlying areas. The result, however, is not a gradual return of these areas to their former complexity. Instead of seeking to foster heterogeneous centers for a mix of users and to offer opportunities to immigrant entrepreneurs, the city's planners are causing them to mimic the suburban milieu across the Hudson River in New Jersey.

The move toward making New York City look more like the rest of the United States, then, results from a confluence of factors. First are the ambitions of property developers and large corporations who see new profit potential in the parts of the city they once had abandoned. Second is the limited vision of these entities, which always tend to imitate their last successful project rather than attempt something new that responds to a different context. Third is the political weakness of groups opposing this thrust. As the mobilizations of the 1960s and 1970s have died and as the public at large has bought the argument that competitive pressure requires the jettisoning and replacement of run-down facilities rather than their upgrading, there is no effective opposition to these plans. Many people are nostalgic for the city of memory, but preservationist efforts are mostly directed toward retaining building facades rather than traditional uses. Lastly, the mind-set of public officials keeps them from seeing logics other than the ones purveyed by developers, corporate directors, and conventional architects and planners and causes them to regard any opposition to their schemes as retrograde. Welcome shoppers, to the Gateway Center at Bronx Terminal Market!

Note

Parts of this essay were drawn from Susan S. Fainstein, "The Return of Urban Renewal: Dan Doctoroff's Great Plans for New York City," *Harvard Design Magazine* 22 (spring/summer 2005), 1–5.

JAUNTY AND DECOROUS

Francis Morrone

The title of this essay comes from Jan Morris's beautifully evocative book *Manhattan '45*, published in 1987. She described the demeanor of Manhattanites in the year the war ended, a time when Manhattan, perhaps for the only time in its history, could claim without hyperbole that it was the "center of the universe." What follows are my thoughts on what has become of the "jaunty and decorous" demeanor of Manhattanites in the last half century or so.

⁕ ⁕ ⁕

The city offers many varieties of public spaces: sidewalks, plazas, squares and neighborhood parks, metropolitan parks, interiors of public buildings, interiors of subway cars and buses, subway stations, escalators and elevators and stairs of various kinds, supermarket aisles, and so on. As city people—as citizens—we are called upon to know how and for what purposes to use each of these spaces. There is an etiquette to their use. For example, on escalators it is customary to stand on the right, walk on the left. On the subway, it is a breach of etiquette to place one's bags on an empty seat, a breach compounded if one fails to remove them before being asked. Both standing on the left on an escalator and putting your bags on the seat next to you in the subway violate tacit compacts about how and for what purposes we as citizens use different kinds of public space.

Cell phones, iPods, and a suburban mentality of isolation have helped insulate New Yorkers from their fellow citizens and have changed the rules and etiquette that once guided one of the central pleasures of urban living: walking.

Another instance of tacit compacts of urban etiquette involves walking on the street. Tacit compacts are a strict requirement if pedestrian flow on Manhattan streets is not to come to a complete halt. In his book *City* (1988), William H. Whyte writes,

> What is most impressive about the individual pedestrian is the skill with which he adapts his moves to the moves of others. The simple avoidance of collision, as Erving Goffman noted, is really a rather remarkable demonstration of cooperative effort.

Whyte wrote about the thousand tacit understandings of pedestrian movement on the sidewalks of New York: the 100 percent conversation, the step-and-slide, and, above all, walking on the right. "Pedestrians," Whyte writes, "usually walk on the right. (Deranged people and oddballs are more likely to go left.)"

An August 2004 *New York Times* article by Ken Belson, "No, You Can't Walk and Talk at the Same Time," though ostensibly about the problems created by pedestrians using mobile phones, was really about the breakdown of these tacit understandings, sixteen years after Whyte's book was published. Here are two key paragraphs:

> There are no statistics on the number of pedestrians injured while talking on cellphones. But Kit Hodge, the campaign coordinator for Transportation Alternatives, a group that advocates for pedestrians and bicycle riders, says the congestion caused by mindless cellphone use on city sidewalks is "out of hand," adding that she has seen shoving matches break out between pedestrians and has herself been smacked by callers who were walking and gesturing wildly.
>
> Still, at least an accidental smack requires two strangers to acknowledge each other. The proliferation of cellphone use on city streets is also contributing to what urban planners have come to call the privatization of public space. Whether they are making calls out of a sense of necessity or as a simple means of escape, cellphone walkers are less likely to help a stranger in need, for instance, or to exchange pleasantries with passers-by. They are effectively cutting themselves off from the random encounters in public spaces that used to invigorate city living.

Fourteen years before Whyte's book, the sociologist Richard Sennett wrote *The Fall of Public Man*, about contemporary society's devaluing of the public realm. Sennett said psychology was to blame. That is to say, psychology in the twentieth century educated the masses to a belief in the primacy of the interior life. Reality, most people nowadays believe, is to be found inside ourselves, or in our intimate associations—Sennett used the term "tyrannies of intimacy." The public realm becomes something to be endured or ignored. As a result, the manners that once sustained the public realm are increasingly being abandoned. The tacit understandings that the sociologist Erving Goffman described in 1956 in *The Presentation of Self in Everyday Life* and that Whyte described in 1988 are eroding with each passing day.

Etiquette books are largely about our "presentation of self in everyday life." Emily Post wrote, in *Etiquette* (1922):

All people in the streets, or anywhere in public, should be careful not to talk too loud. They should especially avoid pronouncing people's names, or making personal remarks that may attract passing attention or give a clue to themselves....Do not attract attention to yourself in public. This is one of the fundamental rules of good breeding. Shun conspicuous manners, conspicuous clothes, a loud voice, staring at people, knocking into them, talking across anyone—in a word do not attract attention to yourself.

By this standard, our public realm is crowded by people conspicuously lacking in "good breeding." For example, who in Manhattan today does not on a daily basis encounter someone talking very loudly into a mobile phone—on the bus, perhaps, or in the aisles of Barnes & Noble? Mobile phones have been around long enough that it's hard to think that anyone doesn't know that you don't have to shout into them to be heard by the person at the other end. Rather, only two things can explain some people's tendency to speak very loudly into their phones. One is that it never occurs to naturally loud talkers to lower their voices when in public. The other is that the person speaking into the phone actually wishes to call attention to himself. Either way, forgetfulness or exhibitionism, we have an absence of good breeding. I have nothing against mobile phones. I own and use one. They are marvelously convenient. But they are a menace in the hands of many people. As for Post's "talking across anyone," it too is an omnipresent phenomenon on mass transit. One regularly encounters people carrying on loud conversations with each other across subway aisles. One cannot imagine such people not knowing they are being rude, but, in fact, I don't think they do know this. But such people, whether unaware of their rudeness or aggressively flouting good manners, exhibit a lack of good breeding.

Now, is good breeding a concept we ought to be promoting? Doesn't it sound elitist or, worse, suburban? I think it is neither of those things and is in fact much more relevant to the urban than to the suburban setting. That is because etiquette is a system—admittedly, at times, arbitrarily conventionalized, like language—that allows, among other things, masses of people in crowded environments, filled with strangers, to get along. Etiquette is the set of customs to which a people tacitly consents and that comes before the law. When etiquette fails to do its job, the law may step in. That is why we have rules of the road for drivers. It is a realm in which we have judged it too great a risk to rely on tacit consent. The law generally lets etiquette control the pedestrian realm. Yes, pedestrians are not permitted by the law to cross streets against the light or to "jaywalk." But the law does not mandate, for example, that pedestrians walk on the right, as the law requires cars to move on the right. Cars move on the right because when the laws were drawn up, nobody questioned that it was just more natural to move on the right, for that was what pedestrians did and what, indeed, many parents taught their children to do. (I do not know if moving on the right is as natural to left-handers as to right-handers. I suspect not. It is also, of course, culturally variable.) What custom mandates is as important as, if not more important than, what the law permits. But custom's mandates are enforceable only through shame. And shame presumes acknowledgment of the existence of other people and in some measure valuing their feelings. The problem today is that we are solipsistic. This, I believe, is caused by many things, one of which, surely, is that we have jettisoned etiquette—good breeding—as an antiquated, antidemocratic notion and substituted for it the concept of "do your own thing." Technology has obliged to make this possible in a degree one might never have imagined.

The British writer Lynne Truss, in her 2005 book *Talk to the Hand*, writes, Sometimes I think we were better off before the term "personal space" escaped from sociology and got mixed up with popular ideas of entitlement. It is now, however, firmly in the *Oxford Dictionary of English*, defined as "the physical space immediately surrounding someone, into which encroachment can feel uncomfortable or threatening."

According to Truss, "it's as if we now believe, in some spooky virtual way, that wherever we are, it's home." This echoes Post: "Do not expose your private affairs, feelings or innermost thoughts in public. You are knocking down the walls of your house when you do."

In February 2006, an article by Linton Weeks, "Burdens of the Modern Beast," appeared in the *Washington Post*. The subject was the extraordinary amount of "stuff" people nowadays carry with them wherever they go. Weeks notes that if you look at old photographs of the city, you can't help noticing that no one is lugging around a satchel bursting with his or her personal stuff. All that baggage gives the antisocial yet another weapon with which to assert their personal space. Few people on the subway even think about taking off their backpacks and holding them at their side so as not to knock into others. To be on a crowded train is to be buffeted by backpacks. Prior to this onslaught of backpacks, which seems to have arisen rather suddenly sometime within the last twenty years, straphangers had evolved a marvelous ability to hold their bodies in such a way on crowded subways so as to avoid any inappropriate contact with another. This ability of straphangers represented one of those group adaptations, based on tacit compacts, that make life in a city possible. It was, indeed, about personal space, but it was the opposite of today, for at one time people protected their own space by respecting that of others and that required being always aware of others. Today, space is maintained by the buffeting action of backpacks, allowing all awareness of other people to disappear. But why so much stuff in the first place? Weeks quotes the cultural critic Thomas Hine, who says all this baggage reflects "the tendency of our society to dispense with sources of shared stability—the long-term job, neighborhoods, unions, family dinners—and transform us into autonomous free agents." It is another example of what Post called "knocking down the walls of your house."

Whither this state of affairs? On the sidewalks of the city, people have lost all sense of those fine gradations of movement that make flow possible, but that require a real sense of the proximity of other bodies. It is, above all, about a false sense of autonomy as atomization, and we see it in paradigmatic form in the suburban cult of the automobile. Defenders of the car, like James Q. Wilson or Randall O'Toole, cite how it has extended individual freedom, something we Americans hold sacrosanct—as well we should. The notion is that the car can take you very many more places than shared mass transportation can and on your own schedule. Being private is also freedom enhancing. You can schlep around nearly as much of your stuff as you wish, fill your space with stereo music of your choosing, chatter away on a (one hopes) hands-free mobile phone, sip occasionally from that grande latte you keep in the cup holder at your side, listen to audio books on the car's tape deck. For moms getting around with kids, the car may be the greatest invention of all time. Many Americans' happiest hours are spent in their cars. The anticar argument will go nowhere until anticar people recognize the very real ways in which the mass of Americans feel the car has vastly enhanced their lives. The single greatest reason for the rise of automotive culture in the United States is quite simply that it is what most people want.

It is the experience that people increasingly are attempting to replicate in the urban environment. It is not TV, it is not the mobile phone, it is not the Walkman or the iPod that has led to the "fall of public man." Indeed, brilliant though Sennett's thesis is, I am not sure it is even psychology and "tyrannies of intimacy," per se, that caused the fall. The proximate cause, as I see it, is the automobile. All the rest represents spin-offs of the driver's auto-atomization. The iPod allows the straphanger to enter car space. The car itself, however, answered a pre-existing need or desire of Americans. Jane Jacobs's diagnosis from 1961 in *The Death and Life of Great American Cities* still holds up. She wrote of the "Radiant Garden City Beautiful," i.e., the compound of the urban-planning visions that sought to meliorate urban ills by making cities less citylike. (I think she was a bit misguided in her condemnation of the City Beautiful, but her point is essentially valid.)

She did not mention, though she did echo, Richard Hofstadter's *The Age of Reform* (1955) with its analysis of the Agrarian Myth that has been (and continues to be) such a dominant theme in American society and politics. Americans borrowed their patterns of urban reform from the British. In Britain the Virgilian ideal of country-house living begat a public-parks movement, exemplified by the designs of Sir Joseph Paxton, which inspired the American Frederick Law Olmsted and the Englishman in America Calvert Vaux. Central Park, a magnificent artifact, was, as it were, a simulacrum of the countryside and wilderness set within the city to ward off the ills of city living as such. When Olmsted and Vaux laid out Eastern Parkway and Ocean Parkway in Brooklyn, they borrowed from Paris, but from the anglicized Paris of the Avenue de l'Imperatrice, a boulevard *sans commerce*, that is to say, a Paris boulevard that did not have shops and cafes and kiosks and advertising signs—or crowds. Just so, American suburbanization has roots in English suburbanization. Suburbia allows Everyman his country-house fantasy. And if the modern suburbia seems the antithesis (which it is) of the real countryside, it nonetheless speaks to that longing in the breast of the average American for his homestead surrounded by green grass and trees. Only via the hypersprawl and the car that made it possible could this fantasy be played out in the democratic fashion that it has. The car has led to a hypertrophied fantasy of the Jeffersonian nation of self-sufficient yeomen. Many environmentalists seek to encourage the development and use of cleaner fuels to mitigate the environmental damage caused by cars. But no fuel can alter the social or political impact of automotive living.

There's a flip side to all this and that is the importation of urban values into suburbia. A March 2004 *New Yorker* featured Malcolm Gladwell's fascinating profile of the architect Victor Gruen, the designer of the first enclosed air-conditioned suburban shopping mall, Southdale, in Edina, Minnesota. Gruen came from Vienna, where he had studied architecture. He honestly believed that in his malls, he was replicating the experience of a stroll on the Ringstrasse. Leave it to a modern architect to believe there is some eternal essence of the Ringstrasse apart from its ornamentation. No matter. The enclosed suburban mall was conceived to be every bit the simulacrum of the city that Central Park was of the countryside. The basic functionality of the mall is that people drive to it and park their cars in vast parking lots. These people then enter the climate-controlled confines of the mall, and they *walk*. They saunter and stroll and kibitz just like (sort of) in the old neighborhood. Old people go there to sit on benches by the fountain to pass the day, just like they did on upper Broadway. Kids hang out in malls, get in trouble in them, go courting in them. Families arrive together, break off on individualized expeditions, and recombine for a tasty meal at the Cheesecake Factory. The enclosed mall isn't a place to zip into and zip out of. It is not a strip mall. It is a total experience, one that is meant to replicate something of city life. Mall managers place great emphasis upon mixing stores cleverly and not allowing dead spaces, on keeping the joint as animated as possible, all while shutting out the weather and the sky. Some commentators, like Witold Rybczynski, go so far as to defend enclosed malls as essentially urbane places. The malls, in any event, are a theme-park-like dash of pedestrian culture in the otherwise antipedestrian realm of suburbia.

The city itself is increasingly being conceived as another mall. Whole neighborhoods, from SoHo in Manhattan to Forest Hills in Queens, are dominated by the exact same chain stores that are found in suburban malls and in other American big-city downtowns. In the immediate postwar years, before many suburban malls had been built, suburbanites came to the city for shopping and dining and for a dose of pedestrian culture. Then, as malls sprang up and as the suburban exodus itself left cities economically distressed, fewer suburbanites came to the city for pleasure as opposed to work and, often, even decreasingly for work. Then many American cities, not least New York, embarked upon ambitious clean-up campaigns so that downtowns could be positioned against malls in the war for suburban consumers' dollars. And it's not just or even mainly suburbanites who tool into the city on a weekend afternoon or evening that we're talking about but the current generation of New York City residents, many who have come from elsewhere in the country. For now that the United States is (as it has been since 1970) a majority suburban nation (the first in history with a majority of people who reside not in cities or in the countryside but in suburbs), a majority of American-born, non-native New Yorkers are the products of suburbia. They are ostensibly in New York as an antidote, at least till they get married, start a family, and return to the dullness of their native suburban habitat. Add them to the people who live in suburbia and come into the city for amusement or edification and then add the other American tourists, most of whom are suburbanites, and at any given moment, the temporary population of the city overwhelmingly comprises people who either now live in suburbia or who have grown up in suburbia. I could well be wrong because I have no hard facts to back up my case, but I suspect that it is this overwhelming suburban presence that has made Manhattan seem a simulacrum of itself, a pod-city (like the pod-people in *Invasion of the Body Snatchers*) version of itself in which the city is an outwardly alluring thing but that, on closer inspection, reveals itself to be more and more off its true nature. And this brings us back to pedestrianism and the fall of the public man—the tacit compacts are breaking down all over the place, perhaps because at any given moment the city streets are dominated by people who have never assimilated the urban etiquette, who have never become urbane.

I admit that is too pat. Many lifelong New Yorkers are as incognizant of urban manners as any suburban transplants. But that is only to say that lifelong New Yorkers are as prey as anyone to the dominant cultural tendencies of our time. In his book *Outgrowing Democracy* (1984), the historian John Lukacs wrote of the "Bourgeois Interlude" in American history, a brief half century—roughly 1900 to 1950—in which American life was "both urban and urbane." (Bourgeois means "city dweller.") During this time, Americans from all over the country aspired to or emulated a Manhattan style of life, or at least what was popularized and glamorized as a Manhattan style of life. It matters little, however, whether the object of Americans' aspirations and emulations was real or make-believe. What matters is that the values emanated from Manhattan and touched the souls of people all across the country—people like the Kansas farm wife staring longingly out her window at limitless fields as the strains of a Gershwin tune came over the radio set in the living room. Toward the close of the Bourgeois Interlude, New Yorkers could be described as "jaunty and decorous," as Jan Morris put it. In the postwar years through to nearly the century's ending, the balance of aspiration and emulation shifted as more and more New Yorkers, that putative bourgeoisie, moved to the suburbs and as fewer and fewer Americans held Manhattan in their hearts. The popular culture—movies, music, TV—registered these shifts with barometric accuracy. Where once people living in the Lower East Side dreamed of living on the Grand Concourse, now people on the Grand Concourse dreamed of living in Great Neck. In other words, city people were likelier to aspire to suburbia than country people were to aspire to the city. In the 1990s, Manhattan's fresh new image was widely heralded. Once again, commentators said, kids from the hinterlands couldn't wait to move to the big city, which they saw charmingly portrayed in *Seinfeld* and *Friends*. But they aspired to a pod-city that was suburban in its core.

Many of our contemporary urban arrangements both reflect and foster the antipublic, essentially suburban attitude. There is a well-known 1948 wide-angle photograph by Todd Webb. (It is beautifully reproduced in a foldout format in the 1988 book *Todd Webb: Photographs of New York and Paris 1945–1960*.) It shows a block of Sixth Avenue, between Forty-third and Forty-fourth streets. It's the west side of the avenue, where 1133 Avenue of the Americas now stands. This gigantic 1969 building (forty-five stories and a million square feet of floor area) was built by Seymour Durst and designed by Emery Roth & Sons (a firm that designed or had a hand in designing fully one-half of all the office space built in Manhattan between 1950 and 1970). The building is a fairly ordinary, gigantic modern office building, which is to say completely uninspiring. The main tower is set well back from the lot line, creating a plaza enclosed on its south and north by the building's projecting wings. Thus it has a plaza that breaks the rhythm of retail frontage, while the wings, intended for retail businesses, were designed not to be showy and, given the economics and the rents that prevailed in the large-scale postwar rebuilding of Sixth Avenue, were and are suited primarily for high-paying (i.e., typically dull) occupants. Today, the southern wing houses the International Center of Photography, a fine institution that nonetheless adds nothing to the street. The northern wing is, I believe, a bank branch. In the middle of the plaza are some plantings. You get the picture. Now Webb's photograph shows something that could not conceivably be more different. It shows a tawdry, ramshackle row of small retail shops in low-rise buildings dating from when the El roared overhead on Sixth Avenue (though the photograph was taken after the El had been dismantled). One clearly discerns all the shops in the photograph. From south to north we see a cigar store, with a tuxedo rental store above it; a small food store; the Silver Rail Bar & Grill; a luggage store, with a typewriter re pair shop above it; a used and collectible record store ("old time favorites, swing, hot jazz, popular, classical, operatic, foreign") with, above it, something called Brown's Talking Picture Operating School (a school for projectionists, perhaps?); a bar called Martin's, with the Spanish American Billiard Parlor above it; Richtone Artists' Materials; *another* used record store (with hard-to-get hillbilly records); a lunch counter; a large back-date magazine store; Sam's Cut Prices ("bargains on all kinds of razor blades"); Irving Men's Shop; and, at the Forty-fourth Street corner, Christy's Healthy Drinks ("100% pure orange juice").

There is nary a plaza or a bank branch or anything other than small mom-and-pop businesses with garish signage proffering a stunning variety of mostly cut-rate merchandise. After the El came down, Mayor La Guardia, in response to his friend President Roosevelt's request that the mayor do something to promote Washington's Good Neighbor policy toward Latin America, renamed Sixth Avenue "Avenue of the Americas" (1945). As the city entered a postwar period of intensive build out of office space, there was, needless to say, vast sums of money to be made on the avenue—by developers, of course, and by the city in increased tax revenues. The powers-that-be gleefully razed the old dilapidated buildings with their cut-rate mom-and-pops. But as with "urban renewal," so with private development of this sort: the vanquishing of the "slums," whether residential or, as here, commercial, was viewed by many (most?) as a sign of inevitable progress.

It was, we all know, anything but progress. Who reading this book does not pine for the days when cut-rate establishments flourished at the peripheries of big-city downtowns? The block Webb photographed was not an anomaly. On every block was a scene like Webb's, broken occasionally by something special like Joseph Urban's Ziegfeld Theatre. In place of the cheap stores rose the gleaming corporate headquarters of J. P. Stevens, Celanese, Burlington Industries, Exxon, Time & Life, McGraw-Hill, J. C. Penney, and Equitable. Fortune 500 corporations do not want messy retail in the bases of their buildings. This is one of the principal areas where the values of giant corporations and modernist architects jibed. Both wanted to do away with anything messy. So did the city, which helped out the corporations and the architects with the 1961 zoning code, which encouraged the creation of pristine, deadening plazas in exchange for increased floor area within buildings. Did I mention that the men and women in Webb's photograph are jaunty and decorous?

The British ideal that guided urban reform in the United States in the time of Olmsted and Vaux was that of *rus in urbe*—the country in the city. Today the guiding ethos is *suburbe in urbe*.

Acknowledgments

This book would not have been possible without the generous support of the Graham Foundation for Advanced Studies in the Fine Arts and its commitment to a creative public dialog around issues of architecture and the built environment. We are also deeply grateful to the J. M. Kaplan Fund for supporting this book (with a Furthermore Grant in Publishing), to City Lore: The New York Center for Urban Folk Culture for administering the grant, and to both of them for their ongoing interest in documenting New York City. We are indebted to Dr. Roberta Feldman for continually inspiring us to look deeper and more fully at the consequences of the built environment. We want to thank Clare Jacobson for recognizing the value of this project and Linda Lee for her excellent proofreading. And special thanks to all the wonderful contributors who so enthusiastically joined this project to explore the rapid changes and resulting challenges facing the city they love.

Contributors

Marshall Berman was born in the Bronx, attended New York public schools, then Columbia, Oxford, and Harvard universities. He is married and has two children. He has received Guggenheim, NEH, and other fellowships. He has taught political theory and urbanism since the late 1960s at CCNY/CUNY as well as at Stanford University, the University of New Mexico, New School University, and Harvard University Graduate School of Design. He is on the editorial board of *DISSENT* magazine. His books include *The Politics of Authenticity* (Atheneum, 1970), *All That Is Solid Melts Into Air* (Penguin, 1982), *Adventures in Marxism* (Verso, 1999), and *On the Town: One Hundred Years of Spectacle in Times Square* (Random House, 2006). He also has published many articles on politics and culture.

Deborah Cowen is a Toronto scholar and activist. She has a PhD in geography from the University of Toronto and is currently a postdoctoral fellow at York University. She won a prize from the Canadian Association of Geographers for her dissertation work and has published in several leading journals. She is cofounder of Planning Action, a group dedicated to working for social justice through activist planning in Toronto.

Eric Darton is a cultural critic and the author of *Divided We Stand: A Biography of the World Trade Center* (Basic Books, 1999). He has lived in New York City and has been observing its vicissitudes all his life. In the late 1970s, as art and performance editor for the *East Village Eye*, he started tracing the transformation of his native city. Darton has also recently contributed articles on urban culture to *Metropolis*, *Culturefront*, and *Designer/builder*. His critically acclaimed novel, *Free City* (W. W. Norton, 1996), has been published in German and Spanish editions.

Susan S. Fainstein is a professor in the urban planning program at the Harvard University Graduate School of Design. She previously taught at Columbia and Rutgers universities. Her teaching and research have focused on comparative urban public policy, planning theory, and urban redevelopment. Among her books are *The City Builders* (University of Kansas Press, 2004) and *Cities and Visitors* (coedited with Lily M. Hoffman and Dennis R. Judd) (Blackwell Publishing, 2003). She is the recipient of the 2004 Distinguished Educator Award of the Association of Collegiate Schools of Planning.

Robin D. G. Kelley is a professor of anthropology at Columbia University and a leading scholar in African-American studies. His books include *Yo Mama's Disfunktional* (Beacon Press, 1998), *Race Rebels* (Simon & Schuster, 1996), and *Freedom Dreams: The Black Radical Imagination* (Beacon Press, 2003).

Katrina Lenček-Inagaki is an undergraduate at Brown University where she studies art-semiotics and comparative literature. Aided by an extensive background in theater arts, she is currently pursuing cinema. In 2005, she interned at Antidote International Films, Inc. and NYI News in addition to creating her own multimedia works. In 2003, her coauthored short film, *In Transit*, was selected for American Movie Classics' Monsterfest. A native of TriBeCa, she ventured uptown to attend The Spence School, where she was one of three editors in chief of the sociopolitical magazine *spark*. You might find her modeling in *Teen Makeup* (Watson Guptill, 2004) or bicycling around Downtown.

Lucy R. Lippard is a writer, activist, and the author of twenty books on contemporary art and cultural criticism and one novel. She has done performances, comics, street theater, and has curated some fifty exhibitions in the United States, Europe, and Latin America. She has been granted honorary doctorates in fine arts from five art schools. She cofounded *Heresies: A Feminist Journal on Art and Politics*, Printed Matter, Political Art Documentation/Distribution, and Artists Call Against U.S. Intervention in Central America. Her most recent books are *The Lure of the Local: Senses of Place in a Multicentered Society* (The New Press, 1998) and *On The Beaten Track: Tourism, Art and Place* (The New Press, 2000).

Francis Morrone is an arts critic who writes a weekly column for the *New York Sun* and whose works have appeared in the *New York Times*, the *Wall Street Journal*, and many other publications. He has written five books, including the acclaimed *Architectural Guidebook to Brooklyn* (Gibbs Smith, 2001), and teaches the history of New York City and comparative literature at New York University's School of Continuing and Professional Studies. He is a Fellow of the Institute of

Classical Architecture & Classical America and is New York's most popular leader of architectural walking tours.

Robert Neuwirth lived in shantytowns across the developing world for almost two years to write *Shadow Cities: A Billion Squatters, A New Urban World* (Routledge, 2005) in which he argues that squatting is a legitimate form of urban development. A native of New York (he made it from Queens to Brooklyn), Neuwirth has written for many publications, including the *Nation, Fortune, Metropolis,* the *Washington Post,* the *New York Times,* the *Village Voice,* and *Wired.* He received a research-and-writing grant from the John D. & Catherine T. MacArthur Foundation to support his work on *Shadow Cities.* Before becoming a writer, Neuwirth worked as a community organizer. He is currently working on a new book that will look at the rapidly expanding informal economies of the world.

Matthew Schuerman is a reporter for the *New York Observer,* covering economic development and commercial real estate. A graduate of Medill School of Journalism at Northwestern University and of Harvard College, he has written for the *Village Voice, City Limits* magazine, the *New York Sun,* and the *New York Times.* He is an adjunct lecturer at New York University's School of Continuing and Professional Studies.

Neil Smith is Distinguished Professor of Anthropology and Geography at the Graduate Center of the City University of New York where he also directs the Center for Place, Culture, and Politics. He won the L.A. Times Book Prize for Biography (2003) for his book *American Empire: Roosevelt's Geographer and the Prelude to Globalization* (University of California Press, 2003). He works on the broad connections between space, social theory, and history. He has been called the "father of gentrification theory." He is the author of many books and more than 140 articles and book chapters. His work has been translated into ten languages. He has been awarded Honors for Distinguished Scholarship by the Association of American Geographers and a John Simon Guggenheim Fellowship. He has held visiting professorships across the world and is an organizer of the International Critical Geography Group. His latest book is *The Endgame of Globalization* (Routledge, 2005).

Michael Sorkin is the principal of Michael Sorkin Studio, an architectural practice with a special focus on the city, and director of the Graduate Urban Design Program at the City College of New York. His books include *Exquisite Corpse*

(Analytical Psychology Club of San Francisco, Inc., 1994), *Wiggle* (Monacelli Press, Inc., 1998), *Variations on a Theme Park* (Hill and Wang, 1992), *The Next Jerusalem* (Monacelli Press, Inc., 2002), *Some Assembly Required* (University of Minnesota Press, 2001), *Against the Wall* (The New Press, 2005), *After the World Trade Center* (edited with Sharon Zukin) (Routledge, 2002), and *Giving Ground* (edited with Joan Copjec) (Analytical Psychology Club of San Francisco, Inc., 1999).

Suzanne Wasserman is a historian and filmmaker. She is the associate director of the Gotham Center for New York City History at the City University of New York Graduate Center. She lectures, writes, and consults about New York City history, especially the history of the Lower East Side. She has published widely on topics such as the Great Depression, Jewish nostalgia, housing, restaurant culture, tourism, pushcart peddling, and nineteenth-century saloons. Her award-winning film *Thunder in Guyana*, the story of her cousin, Janet Rosenberg Jagan, who was elected president of Guyana in 1997, was aired nationally on PBS as part of the Independent Lens series.

Maggie Wrigley is a writer, photographer, and artist who came to New York from Australia in 1984. She has played music, worked in nightclubs, and curated and participated in shows in alternative art spaces. She has been a part of the Lower East Side squatters' movement since 1988 and still lives at Bullet Space.

Amy Zimmer is a New Yorker, born and bred. She is a staff reporter at *Metro* newspaper and the New York correspondent for Public Radio International's program *Pacific Time*. She has contributed to the *Brooklyn Rail* and *City Limits* magazines. Her *Brooklyn Rail* article about a recreation center in Brownsville won the 2004 Independent Press Association's award for Best Article about the Arts.

Editors and Photographer

Jerilou Hammett holds master's degrees in education and in the humanities. She cofounded *DESIGNER/builder* magazine and for the last twelve years has been its managing editor. She is the coauthor of *The Essence of Santa Fe: From a Way of Life to a Style* (Ancient City Press, 2006). Her roots are in New York, where she was born and raised. She comes from a family of Russian Jewish immigrants who arrived on Ellis Island, struggled on the Lower East Side, assimilated over time, and always considered New York the greatest city in the world.

Kingsley Hammett, a descendant of Irish and Jamaican immigrants, was born and grew up in the New York area. His youth was filled with countless arrivals at Grand Central Station, shopping at Washington Market, wandering Radio Row, lunching at the Automat, and watching through peepholes in the construction barricades as the postwar city grew. He is the publisher of *DESIGNER/builder* magazine, holds master's degrees in journalism and in the humanities/history, and is the author of three books on regional furniture and two on architectural and cultural history.

Martha Cooper has documented New York for more than twenty-five years and is currently director of photography for City Lore: The New York Center for Urban Folk Culture. She has done work for many magazines, including *National Geographic*, *Smithsonian*, *New York*, and *Vibe*. She was staff photographer for the *New York Post* for several years and has contributed photographs to more than fifteen books.

NEW
AMSTERDAM
"UNLIKE ANYTHING BROADWAY HAS EVER SEEN!"
THE LION KING
"SPECTACULAR!"
THE LION KING
AIDA

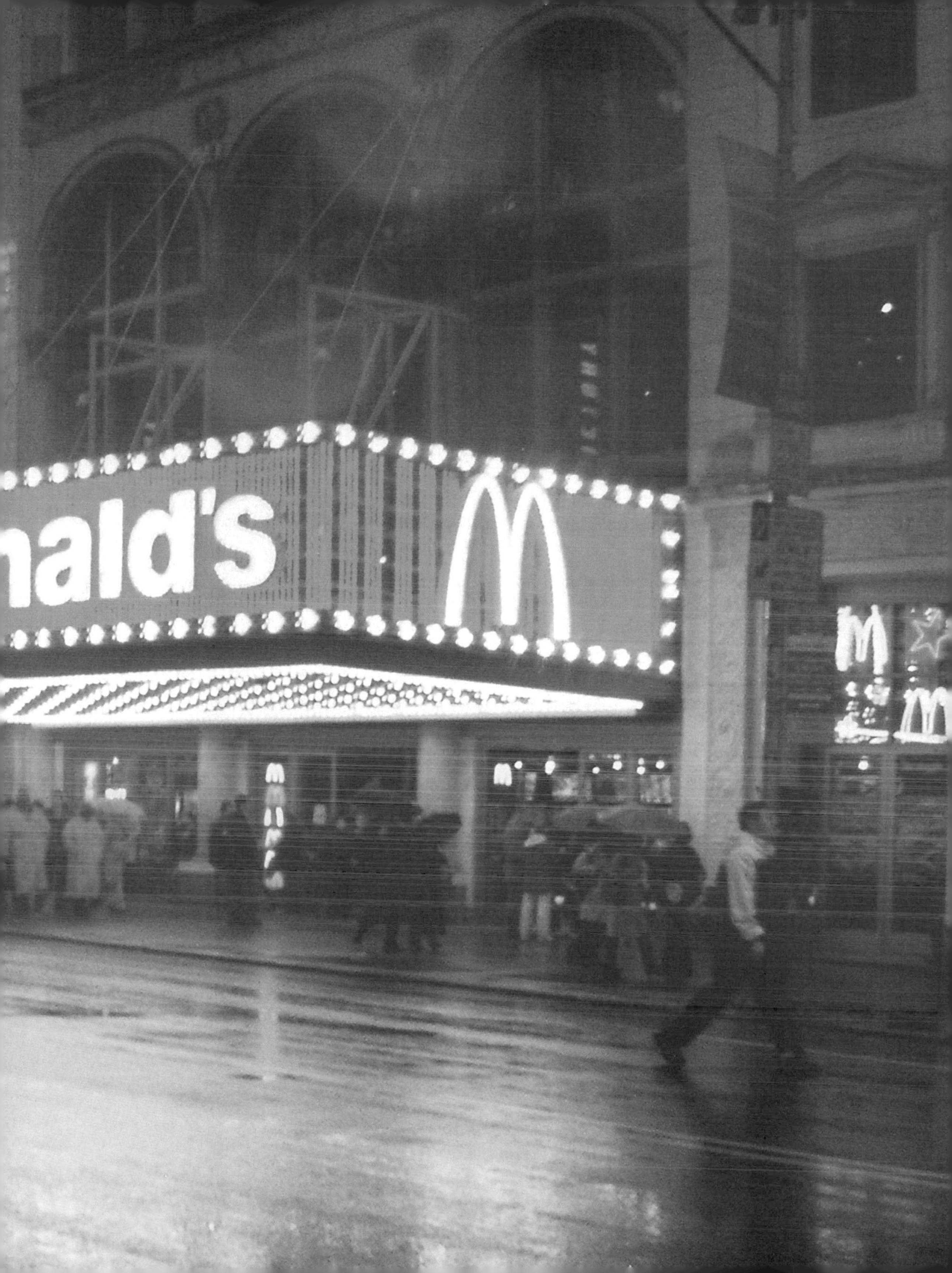
nald's
M